Reliant Sabre, Scimitar and SS1

An Enthusiast's Guide

Reliant Sabre, Scimitar and SS1
An Enthusiast's Guide

Matthew Vale

THE CROWOOD PRESS

First published in 2018 by
The Crowood Press Ltd
Ramsbury, Marlborough
Wiltshire SN8 2HR

www.crowood.com

British Library Cataloguing-in-Publication Data
A catalogue record for this book is available from the British Library.

ISBN 978 1 78500 421 6

Acknowledgements
I would like to thank car owners Shaun Pierce, Guy Betts, John and Richard Valler,
Chris Gallacher, Graham Fradgley, Geoff Richards, Tony and Jaki Heath and John Unwin
for agreeing to be interviewed for this book, and for allowing me to photograph their
cars. A big thank you goes to the RSSOC for help and assistance from the committee
and members, as well as permission to use production figures given in the book. Thanks
also to Dave Poole of 'Sporting Reliants' for some pictures, Graham Walker of Graham
Walker Ltd for technical information and John Adams at racebears.com for his picture
of the SX250. Finally, I'd like to thank my wife Julia and daughter Lizzie for putting up
with me writing yet another book.

Typeset by Shane O'Dwyer, Swindon, Wiltshire
Printed and bound in India by Parksons Graphics

CONTENTS

Reliant Sports Cars Timeline   6

CHAPTER 1   RELIANT AND ITS SPORTS CARS   7

CHAPTER 2   RELIANT'S FIRST SPORTS CARS:
             THE AUTOCARS SABRA (1961), RELIANT SABRE
             FOUR (1961–1963) AND THE SABRE SIX (1962–1964)   19

CHAPTER 3   INTO THE GT MARKET:
             THE SCIMITAR GT (1965–1969)   44

CHAPTER 4   THE FIRST SPORTS ESTATE:
             THE SCIMITAR GTE SE5 (1968–1975)   62

CHAPTER 5   A BIGGER ESTATE AND A CONVERTIBLE:
             THE SCIMITAR GTE SE6 (1975–1986), GTC SE8 (1980–1986)
             AND MIDDLEBRIDGE GTE (1988)   80

CHAPTER 6   BACK TO BASICS:
             THE SCIMITAR SS1 (1984–1989), SST (1990)
             AND SS2/SCIMITAR SABRE (1992)   98

CHAPTER 7   OWNING AND RUNNING A RELIANT SPORTS CAR   114

             Resources   125
             Index   126

RELIANT SPORTS CARS TIMELINE

DATE	NOTES
1934	Reliant formed
January 1960	Autocars MD Yitzhak Shubinsky views Ashley body shell and Ballamy chassis at London's Sports and Racing Car Show and commissions Reliant to build the Sabra
April 1961	Prototype Sabra built and exhibited at New York Motor Show by Reliant
March 1961	Reliant starts production of the first 100 Sabras for direct export to the USA
1961	Autocars starts production of Sabra
October 1961	Reliant takes Sabras number 92 and 93, builds them in right-hand drive, and exhibits them at the London Motor Show (Earls Court) as Sabres
	Reliant Sabre (SE1) with open-top and 4-cylinder Ford engine introduced to UK market
June 1962	Fixed-head coupé version of Sabre Four introduced
October 1962	Reliant introduces the Sabre Six (SE2)
October 1962	Ogle show their SX250 at London Motor Show
September 1964	Reliant introduces the Scimitar GT (SE4) with Ford straight-six engine
October 1965	Ogle Triplex GTS – one-off Triplex glass demonstrator estate shown at Earls Court Motor Show
October 1966	Scimitar Coupé 3-litre (SE4a) introduced with Ford Essex V6
August 1967	Scimitar 2.5-litre (SE4c) introduced alongside lightly improved 3-litre Coupé (SE4b)
1967	SE3 project for Chrysler V8-powered Scimitar Coupé replacement concept in design phase but abandoned due to oil crisis
August 1968	Scimitar GTE SE5 introduced
November 1970	Production of Scimitar Coupé ended
October 1971	Scimitar GTE SE5a introduced
October 1975	GTE SE5a production ends
1975	Longer and larger Scimitar GTE SE6 introduced
1976	SE6a introduced with structural modifications
1979	SE6b with Ford Cologne 2.8 V6 engine introduced
1980	Scimitar GTC Convertible (SE8) introduced
1984	Scimitar SS1 (Small Sports 1) introduced with 1300cc engine
1984	SS1 1600 with Ford XR3 engine introduced
1986	Production of GTE and GTC ceases
1986	SS1 chassis now galvanized
1986	SS1 Ti with Nissan turbocharged 1800cc engine introduced
1987	SS1 gains new Ford 1400cc engine
1989	Last SS1 produced
1990–1992	SST and Mark 1 Scimitar Sabre produced
1993–1995	Mark 2 Scimitar Sabre produced
1988–1990	Middlebridge production of revamped GTE

CHAPTER I

RELIANT AND ITS SPORTS CARS

INTRODUCTION

One of the UK's small independent car manufacturers, Reliant concentrated on niche markets that could be exploited without competing directly with the big boys. The idea was to take advantage of the vagaries of the UK licensing and road tax rules to provide owners with cost-effective transport that was weatherproof, practical and cheap. In the 1930s, that meant small lightweight commercial three-wheelers that were more practical than a motorcycle and sidecar – and cheaper to run than the four-wheeled competition. After the war, the company came out fighting with a new range of vans powered by Reliant's own

design of small 4-cylinder engine. In 1953, the company introduced its first passenger car, the aluminium-bodied Regal; this was followed in 1956 by cars and vans with bodies produced in the new wonder material, glass fibre.

Reliant stood out from the competition as it had its own 4-cylinder 4-stroke engine while the other microcar manufacturers tended to use Villiers single- or twin-cylinder 2-stroke units. While this meant that the Reliant product was usually more expensive, it was also more reliable and cleaner, and could offer better performance. In the 1940s and 1950s, Reliant's lightweight three-wheeled small cars and vans could be driven by someone who held only a motorcycle

Reliant's first foray into the sports-car market was the design and development of the Sabra for Israel's Autocars.

ABOVE: **The prototype Sabra, produced in the early 1960s,
was a neat two-seater with a 4-cylinder Ford engine.**

BELOW: **The Sabra was released on the UK market as the Sabre.
This is the rare soft-top Sabre Six, owned by Tony and Jaki Heath.**

The majority of Sabre Sixes were produced as coupés.

licence, and provided an attractive alternative to a motorcycle and sidecar. Into the 1960s and 1970s, the company produced a range of small three- and four-wheeled cars and vans that were cheap to run both in terms of fuel economy and road tax, and remained Reliant's core business, but the company also developed an unlikely but profitable sideline in producing a range of sports cars, from the early 1960s through to the 1990s.

Despite a historical reliance on small, economical three-wheelers, Reliant now has a long and illustrious record in the production of those sports cars. In view of the company's humble beginnings as a purveyor of small trade-oriented goods vehicles and three-wheeler cars for the masses, the appearance at the 1961 London Earls Court Motor Show of an attractive sports car came as a bit of a surprise to Reliant's customers and competitors. The two-seater Reliant Sabre was based on a project in association with the Israeli company Autocars, known as the Sabra. It came in two styles – an open-top with fold-down hood or a closed coupé – and was initially powered by a Ford straight-four 1703cc unit from the Ford Consul. In 1962 the Sabre gained the 2.5-litre straight-six from the Ford Zephyr and Zodiac range and was renamed the Sabre Six.

Reliant cemented its new car's sporting image with some rallying success, competing in iconic events such as the 1962 Tulip and RAC rallies, and the 1963 Monte Carlo and Alpine events. However, although the Sabre was well received by the press of the day, the car did not sell as many units as expected. It was replaced in 1964 by a totally restyled coupé, the Scimitar, and at the same time Reliant also introduced its first four-seater passenger car for the UK market, the Rebel.

The Scimitar was a two-door coupé with ample room for the two front-seat passengers and a small bench seat behind for a couple of children. With styling by David Ogle Associates, the new coupé was modern in appearance and, utilizing a modernized and lengthened Sabre chassis, provided Reliant with a firm base on which to move their four-wheel sporting range firmly up and into the GT marketplace. With its up-to-date styling and Ford engines, the Scimitar was seen as a smart and stylish coupé and sold in greater numbers than the Sabre. Reliant's next sports car was the Scimitar GTE, which appeared in 1968. This three-door sports estate was responsible for defining and exploiting a completely new market sector – that of the practical sports car.

Based closely on the Scimitar Coupé, but with a new chassis with wider outriggers, to provide a lower seating position and decent space for two rear-seat adult passengers, the GTE had a Ford 3-litre V6 power plant. It was a true Grand Touring car. With its innovative fastback styling, practical three-door design and four proper seats, the GTE was an instant success and proved to be Reliant's defining model through the 1970s and 1980s. Reliant dropped the Scimitar Coupé from the range in 1970, and then moved upmarket with the introduction of a larger and restyled GTE in 1975.

The GTE model was joined in 1980 by a four-seat convertible, the GTC. In 1986, after 18 years in production, the GTE was phased out, along with the GTC. By then Reliant had introduced the Scimitar SS1 (Small Sports 1), a small two-seat sports car designed to address a completely different market from that of the GTE. The SS1 retained Reliant's traditional construction techniques of a steel chassis with plastic bodywork, in this case styled by Italian designer Michelotti. The glass-fibre bodywork was made up of a large number of separate panels and types of plastic, bolted on to the chassis, which was in itself of a complex design, produced by an outside company in Germany. Despite the car having decent performance and excellent handling and roadholding, Michelotti's styling could not be considered a success, and potential customers stayed away. Despite the car's performance being boosted by the fitting of the excellent Nissan 1800 Turbo engine, a major restyle was deemed necessary. This was carried out by William Towns for 1990, resulting in the Scimitar SST. After a final redesign, in 1992, the car was renamed as the Reliant Scimitar Sabre. Sales figures did not justify the car being kept in production, however, and the last Reliant sports car was finally dropped from the range in 1995.

ABOVE: **Replacing the Sabre was the Scimitar, an up-to-date and modern GT car.**

RIGHT: **Probably the best-known of the Reliant sports-car family, the GTE was the first sporting estate car. This is a 1973 SE5a.**

The final members of the Reliant sports-car family were in the Small Sports range. This is one of the last, a 1991 SST owned by Graham Fradgley.

THE BACKGROUND

Reliant came into being in 1934, when engineer Tom Lawrence Williams left Raleigh to pursue his dream of creating a three-wheeled light commercial vehicle that would fit into the niche UK vehicle taxation class between a motorcycle and sidecar and a conventional four-wheeled van. Taxation classes for commercial vehicles in the UK in the 1930s were based around a vehicle's weight and configuration, and there was a significant cost saving in running a three-wheeled vehicle in the under 8cwt (896lb/406kg) class over a four-wheeler of the same weight. In a small workshop in the back garden of his in-laws' house in Tamworth, Staffordshire, Williams produced a prototype three-wheeled van. It was based on a strong steel chassis and was powered by a 600cc JAP single-cylinder 4-stroke engine. The single seat straddled the engine and the front end had motorcycle-based girder front forks to support the single front wheel. A large wooden box body sat behind the driver's saddle and above the chain-driven rear axle, giving a relatively large and flexible load space.

After a few refinements, including the replacement of the handlebars with a steering wheel, premises were leased in Two Gates, Tamworth, and in June

1935 production commenced. With its three-speed and reverse gearbox and unmatched running costs and convenience, the Reliant 7cwt (784lb/355.6kg) Van was an instant success and an open pick-up version was soon offered. However, the vehicle could struggle with heavier loads, so in 1936 a larger and more capable 10cwt (1120lb/508kg) model was introduced, powered by a more powerful water-cooled JAP 747cc 'V' twin 4-stroke engine. The new model also replaced the chain drive of the original van with a propeller-shaft-driven car-type rear axle, and had slightly larger all-round dimensions, as well as positioning the driver on the right-hand side of the cab, making room for a passenger. Even though the increased weight meant a higher tax to pay, the model proved to be even more successful than its predecessor.

Both the 10cwt and the 7cwt models were produced up to the end of 1937. Around this time, a need for more refinement led to an arrangement with Austin for supplies of their Austin Seven engine, an in-line 4-cylinder side-valve water-cooled unit. This led to the introduction of the 8- and 12cwt models in early 1938. Retaining the motorcycle front forks and the van style, as well as the two-seat driver and passenger cab of the 10cwt van, the new 8- and 12cwt models were increasingly successful in the

UK. Reliant was also finding new export markets for the vehicles, selling increasing numbers in various territories, including Australia, South Africa, Latin America and India.

In 1939, Austin discontinued the Seven, and the supply of engines rapidly dried up. Undeterred, Williams decided to design and produce his own engine, and the result was a neat and compact 4-cylinder side-valve unit. Unsurprisingly, the new engine borrowed heavily from the Austin unit, but with some revised dimensions, as well as an alloy crankcase, repositioned distributor, and cast-iron cylinder block and cylinder head, it was sufficiently different to avoid any patent issues. It slotted conveniently into Reliant's existing range as a direct replacement for the Austin unit. A side-valve straight-four displacing 747cc, and with a bore and stroke of 56 x 76mm (the same as the Austin unit), the new engine gave about 14bhp at 3,500rpm. The first of the new engines was produced and tested in September 1939 and a month later the first all-Reliant production engines were completed in the factory. Production was to be short-lived, however, as the Second World War intervened. In January 1940, all vehicle production was suspended and the factory was turned over to war work.

Post-war, production of the range of small commercial three-wheelers recommenced, along with production of the Reliant engine. In 1949, the commercials were joined in the range by Reliant's first passenger three-wheeler, the alloy-bodied Regal.

MILESTONES

An important milestone in the company's history came in 1954, with the introduction of the company's first glass-fibre-bodied vehicle, the Regal Mark III. Glass fibre was a great material from which to make low-volume car bodies: moulds were cheap and easy to make; the material itself was easy to work; it produced a light and strong structure; and it did not require the expensive metal tooling of a steel body or the panel-beating skills of an alloy body. Glass-fibre bodies soon became standard on the whole Reliant range during the 1950s, and Reliant's experience in using the new material played an important role in the company's success thereafter.

Reliant also played a significant role in exporting vehicle technology, starting with the export of complete Regals to Israel through Autocars Ltd of Haifa during the 1950s. This was followed later by the supply of

Reliant's first passenger car was the Regal, which, with three wheels and an alloy body, offered basic but cheap motoring.

semi-knocked-down (SKD) kits. This method was used by a number of countries for a variety of reasons. Some countries imposed high taxes on imported vehicles, but these could be reduced if the vehicle had some local content. Others used the system to kick-start an indigenous vehicle-manufacturing industry. In the case of Autocars, it was a combination of the two that led to the relationship with Reliant, which effectively kickstarted Israel's own car-building capability. There was no tax advantage in producing three-wheelers in Israel, so, as a development of the business, Reliant designed and developed a four-wheeled derivative of the Regal Mark 4 van for Autocars. Powered by a Ford side-valve engine and named the Sussita, the van was supplied to Autocars by Reliant in the form of many thousands of SKD kits over several years. It was followed by the Carmel, a family car design.

The first of Reliant's sports cars, the Sabra, was designed by Reliant in 1960 and 1961 for Autocars and introduced to the US and Israeli markets at the time. Reliant also identified its potential for the home market and built a pair of Sabras in right-hand drive. The model was renamed as the Sabre for the UK market, with the company designation of SE1, and launched at the 1961 Earls Court Motor Show. The Sabre was rapidly supplemented by the Sabre Six, powered by a 6-cylinder 2.5-litre Ford engine. The new Sabre Six, designated SE2, was introduced at the October 1962 Earls Court Motor Show and differed from the original Sabre SE1 in terms of engine choice, front suspension design and styling. Mainly supplied as a hard-top coupé (the Sabre Six GT), but also available as a convertible (the Sabre Six Sports), the Sabre Six had some success in international rallying.

Alongside all the work on the sports cars during the late 1950s and early 1960s, Reliant continued to produce the three-wheelers that represented the main part of its domestic business. Those vehicles were still popular with the British public. The company was also developing a new all-alloy overhead-valve engine to power them, to replace the existing Austin Seven-based side-valve unit. The new engine went on to power the Regal 3/25, which was a complete redesign of the previous Regal model, and would go on to spawn a whole family of cars, vans and pick-ups that were produced well into the 1970s.

Reliant's financial position changed for the better in 1962, when Gwent and West of England Enterprises bought 76 per cent of the company's shares. Run by entrepreneur Julian Hodge, Gwent and West had holdings in finance, merchant banking, engineering and vehicle distribution. Hodge saw Reliant as a good fit with his automotive interests.

At the 1962 Earls Court Motor Show, David Ogle, founder of Ogle Design, exhibited the Ogle SX250, a smart two-door closed coupé based on the Daimler

The Israelis' Sabra was marketed extensively in the USA as a lifestyle accessory. Its quirky looks, unusual leading-arm front suspension and kit-car origins resulted in relatively low sales.

ABOVE: **Reliant's Sabre was a development of the Sabra. This Sabre Six has a 6-cylinder Ford engine and Triumph-based front suspension to make a useful little sports car.**

LEFT: **The Rebel was both Reliant's first domestic market four-wheeler and its first car styled by Ogle Design.**

SP250 sports car chassis. While only two examples of the Daimler-based car were produced, Reliant engaged with Ogle to style its first domestic four-wheeler, the Rebel, and then to modify the SX250 design to fit on the longer Sabre chassis. This project marked the start of a long collaboration between Ogle Design and Reliant; the result was a reworked Ogle-styled body on a stretched Sabre chassis, providing an elegant and stylish 2+2 closed coupé.

Named the Scimitar GT, with the company code of SE4, the new sports coupé was debuted at the 1964 Earl's Court Motor Show and went into production in 1964. After four years of producing the Scimitar GT, Reliant announced the Scimitar GTE,

coded SE5. Styled by Ogle and based on an all-new chassis, this three-door Sports Estate was the car that would carry Reliant's sports range through the 1970s and 1980s. With Royal patronage – Princess Anne was one celebrated owner – and seen as the first 'sports hatch' that showed that a family car did not have to be staid and boring, the GTE proved to be a success. With a reliable Ford Essex V6 engine and proven running gear, the GTE was a car with good performance and handling. It also afforded a good degree of practicality, with its four adult seats and versatile load area accessed through the opening rear window. In typical Reliant fashion, it defined its own market niche, and had no real competitors at its launch.

ABOVE: **The Scimitar was a two-door coupé that replaced the Sabre. Designed by Ogle and engineered by Reliant, it was a successful GT car in the 1960s.**

RIGHT: **The GTE was a development of the Scimitar Coupé, with an all-new chassis and body shell. The sporting estate design would see Reliant's sports-car range through to the 1980s.**

During the 1960s, Reliant had not neglected its core three-wheeler market, and production of the Regal 3/25 commenced in 1962. This featured Reliant's new all-alloy overhead-valve 4-cylinder engine and was followed in 1963 by the car that was to epitomize Reliant in the 1980s: Del Trotter's Supervan, which featured so memorably on the BBC sitcom *Only Fools and Horses*. Sadly, in 1964 Tom Williams, the company's founder and subsequently Managing Director, died after suffering a heart attack at the works and Assistant Managing Director Ray Wiggin was called upon to step into the breach. Reliant had three factories in Staffordshire at the time: the assembly of complete cars was carried out at the

Two Gates plant in Tamworth; engine assembly and casting were done at a plant in Shenstone; and all bodies were produced at Kettlebrook.

In 1969 Reliant bought its main rival in the three-wheel business, Bond Cars of Preston. Production of Bond's 875 was stopped, but Reliant did use the name for an unusual and slightly bizarre entry into the youth market: the Tom Karen-designed wedge-shaped Bond Bug. However, the Bug's price, two-seat configuration, three-wheel chassis and limited luggage space meant that sales were poor and production stopped by 1974 with just over 2,000 produced.

In 1973, the Regal was replaced by the updated and Ogle-restyled Robin, still a three-wheeler but now

SOME MIGHT HAVE BEENS

At the end of the 1960s, Reliant explored a mid-engined sports-car concept using its own 750cc twin-carburettor engine, the FW7. A mock-up of the car was built in 1970, with a wedge nose, sharp lines, pop-up headlights and a pronounced central roll hoop and fixed rear window. It looked similar to Fiat's X1/9 but actually pre-dated the Fiat design by a couple of years. It soon became clear, however, that Reliant's own engine would not be powerful enough and the project was abandoned.

During the mid-1970s Reliant began to look at replacing the GTE. Bertone was commissioned to carry out some styling exercises in a project codenamed SE82, destined for introduction in 1982. The car was a four-seat three-door hatchback with a 106-inch (265cm) wheelbase, longer than the GTE's 103.5 inches (258.75cm). Keen to use a British-built engine, Reliant chose a Rover 3.5-litre V8, and went for the classic Reliant layout of a fabricated steel chassis and glass-fibre body shell, with unequal-length wishbone suspension up front, and a rear axle fitted to a subframe and located by semi-trailing arms. The car's design had progressed far enough for a full-sized version to be completed, albeit without electrics, when the project was cancelled in 1980 following a slump in the high-priced sports-car market. The car was rather uninspiring in appearance, with a wedge nose, and a roofline extending to above the rear wheels, which then sloped down to the tail to give a large hatchback. It actually looked similar to the aborted British Leyland Lynx project of the later 1970s, which was a lengthened TR7 with four seats and a sloping rear hatchback and also sported a Rover V8 engine.

Another 'might have been' was the Stevens Cipher, a design for a small two-seat open-topped sports car by Tony Stevens. It was based on Kitten mechanicals with its own chassis and glass-fibre body, and appeared at the 1980 UK motor show. Unfortunately, the attractive little car could not find a backer and never made it into series production.

The Stevens Cipher was a small sports car designed by Tony Stevens, using Reliant Kitten mechanicals and Stevens' own body and chassis. It never made it into series production.

sporting an opening rear window (just like the GTE) to give it some hatchback practicality. The four-wheeler Rebel was replaced by a similarly updated Kitten in 1975. At the peak of Robin and Kitten production, in 1975, Reliant was producing around 330 cars every week.

Alongside the continuing activity on the three-wheeler front, the sports cars were not forgotten. The GTE grew in both length and width, to become the SE6 variant in 1975, and in 1979 the Essex V6 was replaced by the Cologne V6 in the GTE. The GTE in turn spawned a four-seat convertible version, the GTC SE8, in 1980. Production of both models ceased in 1986. Prior to this date, Reliant had introduced the Small Sports range, with the SS1 in 1300 and 1600cc versions in 1984. The SS range was produced up to 1990, when it was replaced by the simplified and arguably better-looking SST. Production of the SST, renamed the Scimitar Sabre in 1992, ended in 1995.

In 1973, Reliant's parent company was sold to Standard Chartered Bank, and in 1977 Reliant was sold on to J. F. Nash Securities. Within six months, Ray Wiggin had left the company; he was replaced by Ritchie Spencer. Sales of the bread-and-butter Robin had stalled in the first half of 1977, and Reliant was further hit by a scandal over the car's safety, when it emerged that the steering box could work loose, with catastrophic consequences. The matter was raised in the press and on the television, and was even discussed in Parliament in May 1979, forcing Reliant to issue a recall and to strengthen the steering-box mountings. This was enormously costly for Reliant, both in terms of hard cash and reputation, and sales of the Robin were badly affected. Following the drop-off in orders, the Shenstone plant was closed, and around two-thirds of the workforce were laid off.

The last Robin came of the line at the end of 1981, but all was not lost, and a new revamped three-

The second-generation GTE, the SE6, was longer and wider than the SE5, and moved Reliant further upmarket. This is John Unwin's example, parked up at the RSSOC's Berkshire branch's 'noggin' venue, the New Inn at Heckfield.

ABOVE: **The GTE was a four-seat soft-top tourer developed from the GTE. It was a worthy successor to the Triumph Stag.**

LEFT: **The SS1 family was the last of the Reliant sports cars. Styled by Michelotti, the styling was not to everyone's taste.**

wheeler, the Rialto, was unveiled in January 1982. With demand for three-wheelers dwindling, however, production of the Rialto was a mere thirty to forty cars a week. Production carried on through the 1980s, alongside the SS range, but the company was declared bankrupt in 1990, and in 1991 Reliant was bought by Bean Industries. Production continued, with the Rialto even being renamed as the Robin; indeed, the company was profitable through to 1994, when Bean Industries itself went bust. Reliant was bought by engineering firm Avonex, but found itself back in receivership after just a few months.

A final attempt to resurrect the company came in 1996 when a consortium set up by Indian company San Motors, businessman Kevin Leech and ex-Jaguar engineer Jonathan Hayes bought Reliant and the Two Gates plant in Tamworth for £450,000. Although production was resumed with the Rialto/Robin, the SST was not made again, marking the end of Reliant's sports-car line. Kevin Leech subsequently bought out the others in the consortium, and moved Reliant into the premises occupied by another of his companies, Fletcher Speedboats, located in Burntwood, Staffordshire, some 14 miles from Two Gates. A new Robin was produced there from 1999, but problems with type approval meant that production was forced to end in February 2001. Reliant was finally out of business.

CHAPTER 2

RELIANT'S FIRST SPORTS CARS:
THE AUTOCARS SABRA (1961), RELIANT SABRE FOUR (1961–1963) AND THE SABRE SIX (1962–1964)

AUTOCARS SABRA

Reliant's first sports car came into being as a result of the company's collaboration with Autocars of Israel. After getting the Carmel and Sussita saloons into production, through the provision of knock-down kits (NDK) and production technology from Reliant, Autocars cast around for a project to produce a flagship model that would complement its existing range and

spearhead an assault on the lucrative US market. In January 1960, Autocar's Managing Director Yitzhak Shubinsky visited the Sports and Racing Car Show in London. There, he saw a chassis designed by British engineer Leslie Ballamy for either a Ford or BMC engine, as well as a proprietary glass-fibre body produced by Ashley Laminates for the Ford 90-inch (228cm) wheelbase chassis. The Ballamy chassis had a 90-inch (228cm) wheelbase, was a ladder type and featured

The Sabra was Israel's first sports car. Produced by Reliant and Autocars, it was aimed at the US market.

Ballamy's own design of leading-arm independent front suspension, a live rear axle and transverse elliptical springs front and rear. It had been designed to fit the many proprietary glass-fibre body shells that were available at the time. Shubinsky decided that the combination of the Ballamy chassis and the Ashley body should form the basis of the design for a sports car that Reliant would produce for Autocars. He bought the rights to use both the Ballamy chassis and the Ashley body shell; as part of the deal, Autocars would be supplied with body moulds from Ashley and various chassis components from Ballamy.

Design

Reliant took on the Autocars project, developing a production-ready car from the bare bones of the Ashley body and the Ballamy chassis design. This would become the Sabra. It was designed to be produced initially in NDK form, with kits being shipped to Autocars for assembly, and Autocars taking over production of the chassis and body as soon as possible. Its target market was the USA and the date set for delivery of the first models was an optimistic early 1961, when the car was due to be exhibited at the New York Motor Show in April. Reliant's task was essentially to adapt the Ashley body to the Ballamy

chassis, sort out the running gear so that it worked to an acceptable standard and was easy to produce, and deliver a complete, properly integrated vehicle from the assortment of unrelated parts that Autocars had presented. The first job was to re-engineer the Ballamy chassis and its suspension. Unfortunately, as part of the deal with Autocars, Ballamy had already supplied a large number of chassis and suspension components. As far as possible, in order to keep the budget under control, these had to be reused, which resulted in some engineering compromises. Ballamy's chassis was a robust and substantial ladder type, with two parallel longitudinal box sections joined with box-section cross-members. However, there were other elements of the design that were more dubious.

For a start, both the front and rear suspension had to be completely re-engineered. On the original design, the front leading-arm suspension was sprung with a single transverse leaf spring; when the prototype was constructed by Reliant, it was revealed that the arc of the movement of the leading arm was significantly different from that followed by the transverse spring, resulting in the spring breaking almost immediately. Ballamy claimed that Reliant had built the prototype wrongly – it does seem rather unlikely

The prototype Sabra still exists and is owned by Tony and Jaki Heath of the RSSOC.

The Sabra and Sabre Four's front suspension was a leading-arm set-up with coil over dampers.

that someone with Ballamy's experience could have designed something so wrong – but Reliant quickly replaced the transverse spring with a combined spring and damper unit on each side. The bottom mounts of the spring and damper units were positioned on the front of the trailing arm, and their top mount positioned on a revamped upright sprouting from the front of the chassis member. Rubber bushes in the top and bottom shock-absorber mounts allowed for the slight arc of movement from the leading arm.

At the rear, the Ballamy design had the live rear axle mounted on top of the chassis and sprung by an underslung transverse leaf spring, which also located the side-to-side orientation of the axle using spring shackles. Fore and aft axle location was catered for by a pair of parallel trailing links on each side, fixed at

their front to the chassis and splaying out 15 degrees to fix above and below the axle, just inboard of the hubs. Reliant modified the arrangement to gain more positive axle location and better suspension control, while still using existing components, and the rear of the chassis was redesigned with the longitudinal members stepped up to enable the axle to fit underneath.

As on the front suspension, a combined spring and damper unit was fitted to replace the leaf spring, and the top fore and aft link on each side was reversed to run from the axle to the rear of the chassis, to give positive fore and aft location. Finally, the original chassis also had a pair of fabricated outriggers on each side to carry the body shell; these were replaced by Reliant with a single centrally mounted outrigger on each side to suit the modified Ashley body shell.

The pair of large front over-riders, designed to protect the long bonnet nose, made a distinctive feature on the Sabra.

The body moulds supplied from Ashley provided the outer shell and bulkhead, with no floor. It would have been too time-consuming and expensive to re-design the complete body shell to produce a set of mouldings that could be bonded together to give a one-piece item, so the Reliant design used marine plywood panels for the floorpan. These were then bonded to the outer body shell. With the body and chassis sorted and the two parts integrated, the Ford Consul 4-cylinder 1703cc engine was retained but was mated to a four-speed ZF manual gearbox, which drove Reliant's own live rear axle.

The original intent of the project was for Reliant to productionize the design, then for Autocars to start to produce the cars in Israel. However, in order to achieve the twin targets of appearing at the 1961 New York Motor Show and getting cars to Autocars' US dealers in time, the first 100 complete cars were produced by Reliant and then exported directly from the UK to the USA. Production of left-hand-drive cars began in Israel later in 1961, and continued in small numbers through to 1968, when a total of approximately 171 cars were completed.

With the cars being built at Tamworth, Reliant decided that production for the UK market was feasible. Two right-hand-drive units – numbers 92 and 93 – were duly built and then displayed, as Sabres rather than Sabras, on the Reliant stand at the October 1961 Earls Court Motor Show. The cars were then road-registered in the UK (as 7946 WD and 7947 WD) and used as press cars, featuring in a number of road tests and assessments in the UK motoring press.

Chassis Design and Development

Although the Ballamy-designed chassis was extensively reworked by Reliant, it retained the overall ladder-frame layout, with its two box-section longitudinal main rails joined by cross-members and the leading-arm front suspension. At the front, the main rails terminated in a pair of uprights to support the suspension mounts, and carried a smaller rectangular front extension, while at the rear the two main rails swept up to pass over the top of the axle and were attached to a lighter rear extension that carried the rear of the body and the fuel tank. The main box-section rails were 5.5 inches (14cm) deep

The Sabra evolved into Reliant's Sabre – this is Chris Gallacher's Sabre Six.

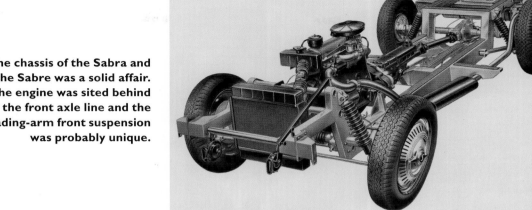

The chassis of the Sabra and the Sabre was a solid affair. The engine was sited behind the front axle line and the leading-arm front suspension was probably unique.

and 2.5 inches (6.35cm) wide, and were constructed from 16-gauge sheet steel. There were two square box-section transverse cross-members in the middle of the chassis, which tied the main rails together. One was below the gearbox tail and the second was positioned where the main rails swept up to go over the axle, with a cut-out to clear the propellor shaft, and three smaller members to form and reinforce the rear box section. At the front of the chassis, forwards of the engine, the main rails were braced with a low mounted tubular cross-member. At the front of each main rail above the tubular cross-member, there was a fabricated upright that carried the top mount of the combined spring and damper unit. A pair of tubular cross-members joined and braced the middle and top of the uprights, and each upright also sported a steel box-section forward extension, which carried the radiator mount halfway along its length. At their forward end, the extensions were joined with another tubular cross-member, and carried the bracketry for the bonnet hinge. As the engine was set well back in the chassis, an open-backed fabricated box was welded to the two upright tubular cross-members to carry a Wilmot Breedon electric cooling fan.

At the rear of the chassis, the main rails were terminated just after the second large cross-member with steel box-section uprights, angled backwards at about 15 degrees to the vertical. This raised the height of the chassis rear to allow the axle to sit below it. An 'L'-section steel plate acted as a cross-member between the tops of the uprights, and from each a rectangular-section steel tube about 2 inches in height and 1.5 inches wide extended backwards horizontally. A central rectangular cross-member was positioned under the extension rails just behind the rear axle line and extended outwards to give an outer body fixing point behind the rear wheels, and the two ends of the extension rails were fixed in place with an open-fronted 'U'-section cross-member.

Body and Interior

The Sabra body was adapted from the Ashley unit, with plywood floor panels bonded to the Ashley upper shell. The original Ashley windscreen surround was considered to be too flimsy and was too vertical for the car, so it was replaced by a new bolt-on windscreen surround that had a steeper rearward sweep, and used the windscreen glass from the Meadows Frisky microcar.

One neat detail was the use of Alfa Romeo Giulietta rear light clusters with the body shell's vestigial rear fins contoured to fit, giving a very clean and well-integrated installation. Steel reinforcement was present in the form of a hoop running up from the 'A' pillars and across the scuttle. The ends of this hoop were bolted to the chassis and the top run of the hoop was indented to clear the instrument binnacle.

ABOVE: **Inside the Sabra and Sabre was a very well-designed and well-equipped instrument binnacle, boasting a comprehensive set of instruments.**

LEFT: **While the boot on the open-topped Sabra and Sabre was not huge, it could carry enough luggage for two.**

A further pair of rectangular-section steel bars were bonded into each side of the rear of the body shell in the inner wheel arches. Visible from the side, these steel bars supported the rear of the body and bolted on to the rear of the chassis. The body shell was bolted to the chassis, so it was relatively easy to remove if required.

The interior of the Sabra was fully trimmed with carpets and had a pair of seats for the driver and passenger, and a small upholstered area behind the seats. The instrument panel and bulkhead were redesigned by Reliant to present the driver with a cluster of instruments in a binnacle, as befitted a sports car of the era. The panel was a separate glass-fibre moulding that stretched across the width of the cockpit. The main instruments – speedometer and tachometer – were positioned in a pair of hooded cowls directly in front of the driver, with a clock between them. The four minor instruments – oil pressure, water temperature, fuel level and ammeter – were grouped in two smaller binnacles under the main instruments. The switchgear was positioned in the centre of the dash, above the ignition switch and heater controls.

The steering wheel was a wood-rimmed Italian-style 'Carlotti' unit with three solid aluminium spokes with an engine-turned finish. The doors had small hinged quarter-lights for ventilation and large frameless manual wind-up windows. Neatly styled door cards finished off the interior of the doors, and the front of the door moulding carried a bulge that helped to integrate the top of the door into the dashboard.

The boot was fairly large but not too deep. It used the space above the rear chassis extension, while the 9-gallon (41-litre) fuel tank sat behind the rear wheels underneath the chassis extension, with the filler on the left-hand side. The spare wheel lived in the boot. The soft top was produced in Vynide, a vinyl material with a leather grain effect, and had a relatively large plastic rear window. The hood was supported on a fold-down steel frame, which was bolted to the car. When up, the hood was secured to the top of the windscreen rail with three quick-release toggle catches, and the hood folded down into the space behind the seats flush with the rear deck, giving the open-topped car a clean and unfussy appearance. A hood cover was supplied to finish off the look, and a full-length tonneau cover was an extra if the driver wanted to protect the car further when driving or when parked with the hood down. The tonneau cover had a full-length central zip so the passenger side could be covered when the car was driven solo.

The bonnet on the Sabra and Sabre was front-hinged and included the wings and nose, giving good access to the engine bay.

Two types of hard top were offered. The first was a bolt-on unit, which simply covered the cockpit, retaining the opening boot and offering better security and weather protection. The second option was a fixed top, which ran the whole length of the car to give a coupé-like appearance. It had 'D'-shaped rear side windows and a large circular rear window. While the roof gave the car a sleek and sporting look, it did not have an opening rear hatch and featured a rather obviously fake air extractor vent on the rear.

The bonnet was a large one-piece moulding that included the wings, centre section and nose. It was hinged at the front, to allow the complete unit to open forwards, giving excellent access to the engine and front suspension – a feature it shared with the Triumph Herald, Spitfire and GT6 family. On the nose of the car there was no wrap-round bumper, but a pair of large and distinctive boomerang-shaped over-riders gave the front end a distinctive and unique appearance. The thinking behind these somewhat extravagant adornments was that, although the long and slim nose on the Ashley bonnet was exposed and vulnerable, there was no practical way to put a blade-type bumper on it. The large and somewhat ungainly 'boomerangs' protected it from the US market's practice of 'touch parking' but did little for the car's appearance. The original Ashley bonnet was modified to incorporate mounting blanks for fitting the over-riders, and the over-riders were made from chromed steel pressings. A pair of pressings were slotted together over a glass-fibre moulding, and the complete assembly was mounted on to the blanks moulded into the front of the bonnet. The over-riders were positioned to allow the bonnet to rest on the floor if the stay was disconnected, to give extra access to the engine bay.

An oval air-intake scoop with a chrome surround from an Austin Westminster was sited in the centre of the bonnet, at the front of a 'power' bulge, feeding air to the carburettor(s). Small round combined side lights and indicator lights were placed outboard of the over-riders and a pair of 7-inch (18-cm) diameter round headlamps sat in recesses in the front of each wing. On the lower front edge of the nose, between the over-riders, sat an oval air intake with a polished aluminium surround, two vertical chrome-plated bars and an aluminium mesh filling the void.

Engine, Gearbox and Final Drive

The Sabra was fitted with the engine from the Ford Consul 375, a 1703cc straight-four overhead-valve unit, which, in standard tune with Zenith downdraught carburettor and 7.8:1 compression ratio, produced 61bhp at 5,000rpm. In the Sabra, the unit was lightly tuned, with some porting work and a free-flow exhaust system, to give 75bhp at 5,000rpm. The engine had a cast-iron head and block, a three main-bearing crankshaft and the head was a reverse-flow design, with the inlet and exhaust manifolds on the left-hand side of the unit. With pushrod-operated overhead valves, and a bore and stroke of 82.6 x 79.5mm, it was a development of Ford's 1951 1508cc straight-four. It was a modern engine with over-square dimensions, which made it amenable to being further tuned.

After the Sabra was launched, some sources claim that the engine was also available in Stage II or Stage III tune, using parts from English tuning firm Alexander Engineering Company Ltd, of Haddenham, near Aylesbury, in Buckinghamshire. The Stage II modifications included a higher compression ratio (up to 8.9:1) and

Chrome-plated 'boomerangs' adorned the front of the Sabra and Sabre; acting as over-riders and bumpers, they were an unusual sight on the otherwise unadorned nose.

**The Sabra and Sabre Four were powered by the Ford
4-cylinder engine usually seen in the Consul.**

a pair of 1.5-inch SU CV carburettors. Stage II gave 110bhp at 5,000rpm, while Stage III gave an impressive 130bhp, again at 5,000rpm, along with torque of 98lb/ft at 2,600rpm. However, an authoritative source, backed up by data in the official workshop manuals, refers to Stage I tune giving 72bhp at 4,400rpm and 95lb/ft at 2,500rpm, and Stage II tune giving 90bhp at 4,400rpm and 98lb/ft at 2,600rpm.

The gearbox was a German ZF close-ratio four-speed and reverse unit with synchromesh on all four forward gears. This box was widely praised in the press of the day for its slick action and all-round usability and was a real asset to the Sabra. The only other production car to which it was fitted as standard was the Lotus Elite Type 14. The gear ratios were neatly stepped, with a reasonably high first gear. The differential was a semi-floating spiral bevel drive unit of Reliant's own design, with a final drive ratio of 3.55:1.

It was joined to the gearbox by a short propellor shaft, 20.5 inches (52cm) long and 2 inches (5cm) in diameter, with a Hardy Spicer universal joint at each end.

Suspension and Steering

The front suspension used Ballamy's original leading-arm design and many of the parts supplied to Auto-cars by Ballamy, but was adapted to use coil over damper units rather than the original design's transverse leaf spring. The base of the suspension's leading arms pivoted on maintenance-free sintered bronze bushes on the chassis and carried the suspension uprights on their other end, along with the bottom mount of the combined coil and damper. The pivot of the arm was angled at 38.5 degrees to the fore and aft axis of the chassis, to give the wheel movement somewhere between that given by a forward-facing parallel radius arm and a simple swing axle. The hub

ABOVE: **The leading-arm front suspension gave some interesting and somewhat extreme camber changes to the front wheels if all the suspension movement was used.**

BELOW: **At the rear, the Sabra had a lower forward link and an upper rearward link to locate the axle, and a combined coil spring and damper.**

carriers, kingpins, front hubs, disc brake brackets and discs were sourced from the Standard Vanguard. With the Girling-supplied coil over damper units the suspension had total wheel movement of about 5 inches (12.5cm), evenly distributed between full bump and rebound. The front-wheel movement provided by the set-up was about the equivalent of a swing axle geometry, with pronounced changes of camber at the extremes of wheel travel.

At the rear, the suspension used Girling coil over dampers, which were mounted on a bracket on each outboard end of the axle and bolted to brackets on the top of the rear chassis uprights. Fore and aft and longitudinal location of the axle was achieved with two splayed fore and aft arms at each end of the axle, generally known as 'Ballamy-Reliant' links. The links were rubber-bushed at each end, and were mounted on a bracket one above and one below the axle; the top link went backwards and was bolted to the rear chassis extension, while the bottom link was routed forwards and was bolted to a bracket on the outside edge of the longitudinal member of the chassis. Both front- and rear-facing links were angled outwards at 15 degrees to the fore and aft axis of the chassis, and the combined effect was to create a Watts linkage.

While the set-up worked reasonably well, it could only accommodate any rolling of the car by the flex

of the rubber bushes of the links. This meant that the whole axle acted as a roll bar in extremis, which could result in the inside wheel lifting and inducing rear-wheel steering. Enthusiastic use would put excessive strain on the axle as a whole, which could result in the axle tubes parting company from the differential carrier. As on the front, there was 5 inches (12.5cm) of total suspension movement.

The steering system adopted for the Sabra had to take into account the unconventional front suspension.

The original Sabra front suspension: the front of the leading arm can clearly be seen, as well as the coil over damper.

A standard rack-and-pinion or ball-and-peg system would not work, as the 38.5-degree skewing of the leading arms meant that, as the suspension moved up and down, the steering arm described a complex three-dimensional arc in relation to the chassis on which the steering mechanism was mounted. The problem was sorted by using a vertical bell crank operated by a single Reliant-built rack-and-pinion driven from the steering wheel, which was mounted rigidly on to the chassis. This rack-and-pinion operated a central idler, which conveyed the steering movement to the wheels via a tie rod. This had two arms connected to it, which ran to the front steering arms mounted on the hubs. The system helped to compensate for the movement of the hubs and hence the steering-arm positions relative to the chassis.

While this system did work, it was subject to considerable reactions from the movement of the hubs, so a steering damper was also incorporated into the design, which acted directly on the end of the tie rod. The steering was reasonably high-geared, at two and a half turns lock to lock, and, because Reliant recognized the fact that the unusual front suspension would cause a degree of kick-back and bump steer, a shim-adjusted damping unit was also incorporated into the

mechanism. The intention was to mask the unwanted characteristics and the result was a rather dead feel to the steering and a lack of self-centring.

The whole suspension set-up was sprung fairly hard, so the car showed very little roll while cornering. This was viewed favourably by contemporary road tests. The car exhibited high cornering forces and relatively benign understeer when the tyres started to lose grip, and there were no untoward characteristics if the throttle was lifted during cornering. However, the full range of wheel movement did produce significant camber changes to the front wheels, which did not give ideal suspension geometry in certain circumstances, for example, when one of the front wheels was deflected by a bump in the road.

Brakes and Wheels

The Sabra was fitted with 15-inch diameter bolt-on steel wheels as standard and had the option of centre-lock wire wheels. From the factory, the car was equipped with 155x15 radial tyres. The steel wheels came with ornate polished aluminium wheel trims, which were designed to look like knock-on units, but merely covered the conventional four bolt fixings for the wheels beneath. The brakes were supplied by

ABOVE: **A factory shot showing the Autocars Sabra outside the factory.**

BELOW: **An interior view of the Autocars factory, showing a number of completed Sabras, a soft top, two Coupés and a hard top, as well as Autocars Sussitas and Carmels on the track.**

Girling and were hydraulically operated, with discs up front and drums to the rear. The front discs were 10.5 inches in diameter and the twin opposed piston calipers were both sourced from the Ford parts bin, and were common to the Ford Corsair, Consul, Cortina GT and Lotus Cortina, as well as the Austin Healey 3000. At the rear, the drum brakes were 9 inches in diameter and 1.75 inches in width, and used Austin A60 shoes. The hand brake was cable-operated from a lever on the side of the transmission tunnel and operated on the rear drums.

Development and Production

Production of the Sabra started in 1961, with the majority of the first year's cars being completed by Reliant in Tamworth. Most of these were exported directly to Autocars' US distributor. Reliant completed 162 left-hand-drive Sabras between 1961 and 1963, and at the same time production was also carried out at Autocars' Haifa works, until the middle of

THE SABRA PROTOTYPE

The prototype of the Sabra still exists and at the time of writing was owned by the RSSOC Sabra and Sabre Registrars Tony and Jaki Heath who bought it in 2010 after it had been restored to a good standard by the previous owners, Keith Healey and Hugo Holder. With its Reliant Regal van rear axle, Ford Consul 4-cylinder engine, Meadows Frisky windscreen and surround, and featuring the original Ballamy chassis, which was modified by Reliant at the time to feature coil over damper suspension units, the prototype formed the basis for the production Sabras. Indeed, it is an important car in its own right. There are two notable departures from the production cars. At the rear, the axle sits above the chassis, while in the production cars chassis rails were raised to allow the axle to sit underneath them. Up front, the steering uses an ingeniously positioned MGA lever-arm damper as a bell crank and damper, rather than the production car's simpler set-up, which has a friction damper.

The car was one of those displayed at the New York World Trade Fair of 1960. It had been broken up by the factory later that decade, but somehow survived, to be pieced back together eventually by Keith Healy in the 1980s. Intending to use the car, later owner Hugo Holder converted it to right-hand drive and replaced the original three-speed Consul gear box with a Ford Sierra Type 9 five-speed unit. Since Tony and Jaki Heath bought the car, they have replaced the old wiring with a professionally built loom, and have sorted out the interior, with retrimmed seats, new carpets and a new dashboard. A new glass-fibre transmission tunnel has replaced the crude and ill-fitting sheet-steel version that was on the car when they bought it. Following many glass-fibre repairs to the original body shell, a full respray completed the work. The colour is close to BMC's Iris Blue, the colour in which the car was painted when it was first restored in the 1980s. Research by Tony indicates that the car may have been a darker blue when it was first built, but there are no definitive records of the build, and all the pictures of the car at the New York show are in black and white, making it impossible to determine the actual shade used.

Over the years, Tony and Jaki have continued to use the prototype, and have made several long continental tours in it as well as going all over the UK for RSSOC events. On the road, they find the car is happy to keep up with modern traffic, and cruises nicely at motorway speeds, thanks in part to the five-speed box, although the engine needs to be revved a bit to compensate for a lack of low-down torque. The roadholding and handling are pretty good and, while the steering is somewhat heavy and 'dead', the car is quick to turn in and feels a lot nimbler than the Sabre Six. Essentially Tony and Jaki find that the car is easy to drive and relatively comfortable to tour in, although boot space is very limited!

1963, when the Mark II was introduced. The Mark II Sabra featured a number of small modifications to the rear end, including the adoption of the rounded rear wheel arches and Austin A40 rear light units as seen on the Sabre Six, a smaller indent around the fuel filler aperture in the left-hand rear wing, and a larger number-plate plinth. At the front, the bonnet and body tub were altered slightly to give a small flare to the wheel arches. Mechanically, the cars remained the same as the previous models, although twin SU carburettors were offered.

Production of the Sabra by Autocars ran through to 1968, but the target US market was less than keen, with just forty-one cars from the Autocars production line being exported there between 1962 and 1964,

when exports to the USA ceased. Oddly, from 1964, exports to Belgium soaked up most of the limited production, with sixty-eight cars going to that market out of the 171 produced in total by the Israeli concern. Other markets taking small numbers of Autocars' production included the home market in Israel, France, Italy, the Netherlands and Switzerland.

THE RELIANT SABRE FOUR SE1 OF 1961–1963

Reliant's first home-market sports car grew out of the Sabras that the company was producing for Autocars. Retrospectively known as the Sabre Four, after the introduction of the Sabre Six, the Sabre

LEFT: **One of the two Sabre prototypes exhibited at Earls Court, 7947 WD is in the hands of the Valler family and soon to be restored.**

BELOW: **The rear end of the Sabre prototype had a neat boot lid, vestigial fins and a pair of Alfa Romeo rear lights.**

was a straight copy of the Sabra, apart from being right-hand drive. The car retained the Sabra's unique leading-arm front suspension, Ford Consul 4-cylinder motor and four-speed gearbox of the Israeli cars, and was initially offered as a soft top, swiftly followed by the coupé version.

The UK-market version of the Sabra broke cover at the October 1961 Earls Court Motor Show, when Reliant displayed a brace of 'Sabre Four Sports' cars and a rolling chassis on its stand. These two complete cars were actually originally intended to be Sabras, numbers 92 and 93. Inspection of the original two cars shows that they had been manufactured as right-hand-drive models, and were not converted left-hand-drive examples, and that they had an all-new bulkhead that included reversing the layout of the scuttle area. The new right-hand-drive cars were renamed 'Sabre' and at the show were exhibited along with a bare right-hand-drive chassis. After the show, the two show cars were registered in the UK as 7946 WD and 7947 WD, and were used as press cars. Both cars still exist and are currently owned by the Valler family.

Accommodating the right-hand drive involved significant work on the body shell in the scuttle area, with the battery being moved from the right-hand side to the left, and the pedal box, wiper motor and the other ancillary components being repositioned on the right, making the scuttle area of the Sabre a mirror image of the Sabra. The instrument panel moulding was also new, retaining the Sabra's binnacle and layout but reversed. The scuttle's steel reinforcement behind the dash also had to be changed to run round the new position of the binnacle. Mechanically, the car retained the Sabra's bell crank steering, with a repositioned rack to meet up with the steering column's new position.

Road tests of the Sabre in the UK motoring press were generally favourable, with *The Motor* magazine expressing surprise at the lack of roll and the generally good handling characteristics. The only negative comments tended to relate to the weatherproofing of the cockpit, the low gearing and the occasional jerking of the steering wheel, combined with a lack of self centring. *Autocar* magazine also picked up on the roll-free ride, along with the unfavourable steering reactions, but both magazines were generally quite

complimentary. The positive response from the press encouraged Reliant to believe that the car had a future in the UK market and production was put in hand, with forty right-hand-drive cars completed in 1962 along with thirty-seven left-hand-drive units for various overseas markets. Production fell off in 1963, with only thirty-four cars completed, only one of which was in right-hand drive, before production turned to the Ogle-styled Scimitar.

On sale for three years (1961–1963), the Sabre Four sold in relatively small numbers, although records show around 217 examples (ninety-seven in 1961, seventy-seven in 1962 and forty-three in 1963) being produced at Tamworth in total. However, the bulk of the first and third years' and much of the second year's production comprised Sabras for Autocars (162 cars), for direct export to the USA, rather than Sabres for the UK market. Rumour has it that an additional fifty kits of parts were produced during these three years for export to Autocars, but, mysteriously, the existence of these kits cannot be verified. In all, Reliant produced forty-four complete right-hand-drive Sabre Fours for the UK market between its introduction and the ceasing of production in 1963.

During this time, the UK-built Sabre Fours were subject to limited development. While the mechanical elements remained the same, from June 1962 Reliant offered a fixed-head coupé body option, based on the unit used on the Sabre Six; in addition, a shortened nose bonnet moulding, without the distinctive 'boomerangs', was adopted in June 1963.

THE RELIANT SABRE SIX SE2 OF 1962–1965

With the Sabre Six, which was introduced in October 1962, Reliant built on the Sabre's reputation for rugged and reliable performance by adding a Ford straight-six 109bhp engine taken from the Zephyr and Zodiac models. This, with an additional 36bhp over the 4-cylinder unit, gave the car a welcome performance boost over the Sabre Four. A new four-speed gearbox from the Ford Zodiac was fitted, replacing the expensive ZF box that had featured on the Sabre Four. The Ford gearbox allowed for the fitting of an overdrive unit, which was electrically operated using a switch on the transmission tunnel.

The Sabre Six had a good few inches cropped from its nose to give it a more modern appearance; the change also meant that a proper bumper could be fitted.

The longer engine meant the steering rack and bell crank mechanism had to be relocated ahead of the axle line. The chassis was also modified, with a 'X'-shaped centre reinforcing member to clear the new Ford gearbox and two new body mounting outriggers, and the front extension was widened to accommodate a larger four-row radiator.

To mark the new model out and distinguish it from the Sabre Four, which remained in production alongside the Sabre Six, Reliant set about a major restyle of the existing body shell. At the front, the nose was shortened by around 7 inches (18cm) and a flat front face was introduced, which carried a two-part grille flanked by a pair of combined side and indicator lights sited below the headlamps. The new nose meant that the 'boomerang'-style over-riders could be replaced by a conventional chromed-steel bumper, with a pair of normal over-riders flanking the number-plate mount. The front end was very different in style from that of the Sabre Four/Sabra, presenting an attractive and up-to-date appearance, with a distinct resemblance to Triumph's Mark I Spitfire and the MGB that was soon to appear. The small power bulge of the Sabre Four morphed into a much longer and wider affair on the Sabre Six, but lost the attractive chrome-trimmed air intake at its front. At the back end, the body changes were more

subtle – the wheel arches were rounded off, the rear end of the car was cut off to give a flat rear panel and new rear light clusters from the Austin A40 replaced the expensive Alfa Romeo items. While the Sabre Six was available in open-topped or closed versions, only two open-top cars were produced, with the majority being fixed-head coupés.

The coupé featured a fastback-style roof, moulded on to the body, which had 'D'-shaped side windows, a large rear window and a curious dummy roof vent that was obviously not functional. The rear window differed significantly from that seen on the Sabre Four coupés, with a neat bottom cut-off, and was neatly integrated into the design, losing the circular and ungainly lines of the Sabra's rear end. While Reliant planned to fit the revised body to the Sabre Four, it appeared that only the last eight cars had the new bonnet, and the majority of the later Sabre Fours were drop-heads.

While the two drop-head Sabre Sixes had a conventional boot lid, the coupé version had a spare wheel locker, which was positioned under the rear of the cabin floor. Access was provided by a removable door in the flat vertical rear section of the tail. The locker door was held in place with a pair of escutcheon locks, the spare wheel slotted horizontally into the space, and a wheel-shaped extension on

ABOVE: **The soft-top Sabra/ Sabre hood was neat and easy to use – and it looked OK when up!**

RIGHT: **There was no boot as such on the Sabre Six coupé, just a narrow locker to carry the spare wheel and tools.**

the inner face on the door kept it in place. There was room for the jack and tools down each side of the wheel. Actual luggage space was provided for inside the passenger compartment on the rear deck above the spare wheel well, but, as the rear window was fixed in place, the only access to the space was through the cabin – after folding the seats forwards. The rest of the interior was identical to the Sabra and Sabre Four, retaining the comprehensive instrument binnacle with its full set of gauges and the generally decent levels of trim and fittings.

Once production of the Sabre Six got under way, in 1963, the heavier engine and the increased performance of the cars quickly brought into stark focus the deficiencies of the leading arm front suspension. With the car being much more nose-heavy, the somewhat extreme changes in the front camber of the front wheels, caused by the leading-arm front suspension with its swing axle geometry, gave

rise to unacceptable handling problems. The cars suffered from heavy steering, severe kick-back and poor roadholding, and, after the first eighteen cars had been built, the front suspension was completely reworked. Reliant raided the Triumph parts bin – picking Alford and Alder's modern twin-wishbone unit, as used on the Triumph TR4 – and modified the chassis to accommodate the new set-up. The chassis revisions were relatively minor – basically a beefing-up of the existing front towers and fitting the mounting points for the wishbones on them. The sloping plate with the indents to fit the leading-arm units remained in place on the chassis and are clearly visible on all the Sabre Six chassis, as well as being carried forwards on to the Scimitar GT chassis.

With top and bottom wishbones supporting an upright, which pivoted on a ball joint up top and a brass trunnion at the base, and a decent-sized disc brake, the new set-up was streets ahead of the

The Sabre Six's interior was the same as that of the Sabra – its nicely designed instrument binnacle placed all the instrument in the driver's sight line.

After the first eighteen Sabre Sixes were built, the leading-arm front suspension was replaced by a conventional double-wishbone set-up taken from the Triumph parts bin.

previous one, giving the Sabre Six safe and predictable handling. The improvement was compounded by the replacement of the bell crank steering system, which had been dictated by the leading-arm system, by a conventional rack-and-pinion system from the Triumph Herald. The members of the press were also pleased to see the back of the old 'flailing-arm' suspension, which they had always treated with suspicion, and tended to damn with faint praise – the usual view expressed was that it seemed to work better than they expected! The improvement to the suspension was such that, over the years, many of the first eighteen Sabre Sixes have had their leading-arm unit replaced by the later wishbone set-up.

At the rear, the Sabre Six sported the existing fore and aft linkages seen on the Sabre Four, retaining the advantages and disadvantages of the Sabra and the Sabre Four.

The resulting car was a good sporting coupé and featured in a number of works-supported rallies. With its lusty straight-six engine, its performance was good, and the new wishbone front suspension – fitted from the nineteenth car onwards – gave decent handling and roadholding. As a sports car, the Sabre Six could be considered to be a success, but in the market it was not; sales were disappointing, with a total of only seventy-seven built during the three years of production (1962 to 1964). Competition

from the likes of MG, Triumph, Sunbeam and Austin Healey was overwhelming. Reliant was unable to benefit from the economies of scale that the larger manufacturers enjoyed, putting the Sabre at a serious price disadvantage.

SABRE WORKS COMPETITION HISTORY

The Sabre was the only member of the Reliant sports car family to have been used as a works or semi-works competition car. The first venture into the world of motorsport was the entry of a Sabre Four into the 1962 Tulip Rally. The car, 15 CUE, completed the course but had actually officially retired, as the driver, Peter Easton (who was also Reliant's Public Relations Consultant) had fallen ill.

Despite this setback, Reliant was encouraged by the Sabre's performance and set its sights on the next event, the 1962 RAC Rally, the UK's most prestigious event in the rally calendar, held in November. Three Sabre Four coupés were prepared by the factory and entered, 15 CUE being joined by 6 EUE and 7 EUE. In addition, an open-topped Sabre Four, 42 ENX, was privately entered by Bob Aston from Mintex, the brake manufacturer, with some factory assistance. Two of the factory cars failed to finish – the axles gave up due to the suspect rear suspension

CHRIS GALLACHER'S SABRE SIX

Chris Gallacher bought his Sabre Six, 232 GUE, in 2001, when he was looking for a car that was out of the ordinary to pursue his passion for historic road rallies and the occasional sprint and hillclimb. He already owned a Scimitar Coupé, so a Reliant was of interest, and he was also familiar with the Sabre's reputation as a tough and reliable rally car. When the late Don Pither's car came up for sale, Chris jumped at the chance to own it. Don was a lifelong Reliant enthusiast and Sabre owner, who had not only written several books on the marque, but had also been the founding chairman of the UK's Historic Rally Car Register (HRCR) and had campaigned the Sabre between 1987 and 1995 in many historic rally events in the UK and Ireland. He had changed the car's original registration number, BRP 187B, to 232 GUE, to echo the works cars registrations of 648, 649 and 650 GUE.

The car is a later Sabre Six, fitted with the revised chassis and wishbone front suspension, while the back end has been modified to a Scimitar-style set-up featuring twin trailing arms and Watts linkage. The engine is the original straight-six Ford, but during Don's ownership it had been fitted with a new cylinder head from period tuner Raymond Mays, and a pair of SU HS6 carburettors. The gearbox is now a Ford four-speed, with a Laycock De Normanville J-type overdrive as used on the Scimitar. When Chris Gallacher bought the car it was in good condition, but he has been fettling it ever since, to make it reliable for daily driving and competition use. It is now in such great shape that he has complete confidence in it and is happy to take it around the M25 in rush hour in July, knowing it will cope with extreme conditions and get him home safely. Of course, the fettling of such a classic never ends – Chris has recently converted the car to negative earth and fitted an alternator, and has retissued and resprayed the car in red with white stripes so it just as it was when Don Pither was competing in it.

**Chris Gallacher has owned his Sabre Six since 2001 and uses it
as a historic rally car, competing in events in the UK and abroad.**

Chris really enjoys driving the Sabre and finds the performance impressive. It has a top speed of around 100mph (160km/h) on the track and is exhilarating and exhausting to drive at that point, with everything doing a 'shake, rattle and roll' and battering the senses. The car is great cruising on the motorway or on A roads at the speed limit, where there is still plenty of performance in hand. It runs on 195/70R15 Vredestein Sprint Classic tyres, and the handling is good, but a bit nose-heavy, with understeer making it tend to plough on a bit when pushed. As the car is relatively small and light, it does get buffeted by lorries on the motorway, but Chris finds that the overall roadholding is pretty good.

In the late 1960s, the service manager for Goodyear's Racing Division, Bruce McLaren, and Denny Hulme took the car around the circuit at Goodwood, costing the owner two new rear tyres after each driver had done a flying lap! To thank the owner for this indulgence, McLaren presented him with a McLaren Racing Team pin badge, which Chris Gallacher still owns and keeps with the car as an important part of its heritage.

The car was bought to be used, and its owner has taken it on a number of Classic Marathons, including the 2002 London–Prague, the 2003 Paris–Pamplona and the 2006 Slovakia/Czech Republic, as well as the 2004 Le Jog (Land's End to John O'Groats) touring trial, clocking up over 40,000 miles. Chris relishes the considerable challenge involved in preparing a car that is fifty-plus years old for such outings, finding it very satisfying as an engineer, especially as he (and his navigator) have managed to have finish every event. Chris thinks that his favourite so far was the 2004 Le Jog, held in December and presenting the greatest challenge of all those entered – as well as an opportunity to see some wonderful parts of the UK that he would never normally visit.

Chris's Sabre Six is a nicely sorted, reliable and dependable
steed, with an impressive performance and history.

**The works rally Sabre Four, 42 ENX, is currently
owned by the Valler family and is in fine fettle.**

geometry – but the third works car came in thirty-eighth, and Bob Aston finished thirty-fourth.

The next outing for the three works cars was the 1963 Monte Carlo Rally, with 6 EUE, driven by Derrick Astle and with Peter Roberts navigating, coming in third and 7 EUE (driver Tony Fischer and navigator David Skeffingham) coming in fourth, both in the 2-litre class. With the more powerful Sabre Six now available the last rally for the works Sabre Four was the 1963 Circuit of Ireland event, with Tony Fisher (driver) and Ron Crellin (navigator) coming third in class.

The works team was allocated four Sabre Sixes, three for rallying and one for road racing, which was intended to be entered into the Le Mans 24-Hours race. The new cars had the leading-arm suspension replaced by the new TR4-based system and were first entered into the June 1963 Alpine Rally. One car (648 GU, driven by Jimmy Ray and navigated by Peter Roberts) retired and the remaining two finished twentieth and first in class (649 GUE, with Bobby Parkes driving and Gerry Cooper navigator), and 22nd and second in class (650 GUE, with Roger Clark driving and Bob Aston navigating).

All the works cars failed in the following rally, the August 1963 Sofia–Liège Marathon de la Route, with the rough terrain punishing the cars and their crews badly.

The next big challenge was the November 1963 RAC rally, in which two cars were entered: 649 GUE, driven by Bobby Parkes with Roy Dixon navigating, and 650 GUE, driven by BBC television presenter Raymond Baxter with Ernest McMillen navigating. Baxter crashed out after having a tyre burst and Parkes and Dixon finished third in the GT class. The next outing for the works cars was the January 1964 Monte, where 649 GUE, crewed by Bobby Parkes and Arthur Senior, demonstrated the Sabre's robust build by coming off the road and driving over a seventy-foot cliff. Although this resulted in the car retiring, Parkes and Senior survived with only cuts and bruises. Graham Warner and Peter Roberts in 650 GUE finished fourth in class and ninety-fourth overall. The final outing for the works cars came in the January 1964 Welsh Rally, when 648 GUE was entered with Bobby Parkes and Peter Roberts as the crew, and came in second in class and fourteenth overall.

ABOVE: **The Sabra's defining feature – the front over-riders. This example from Belgium was at the RSSOC Sabra/Sabre meet in 2017.** DAVE POOLE

RIGHT: **Where it all began – the Sabra prototype, still on the road and in the capable hands of Tony and Jaki Heath of the RSSOC.**

The fourth works Sabre Six, the Le Mans entrant 876 HWD, had not been accepted for the 1963 endurance event. While all the rally activity was going on, it was used by Bobby Parkes as a hillclimb car, where it achieved considerable success due to its light weight and powerful engine.

Despite its reasonable results in motorsport and hillclimbing, the limited sales achieved by the Sabre, and the imminent announcement of the new upmarket Scimitar GT, meant that works support for the model ended in January 1964.

SUMMARY

While the Sabra and Sabre may not have achieved the sales success that Reliant and Autocars had hoped for, the cars did give Reliant a foothold in the UK's sports-car market and set the scene for the much more successful Scimitar range. The early cars exhibited some interesting and unconventional engineering practices with the leading-arm front suspension and rear axle fittings, which could be described uncharitably as solutions looking for problems.

SABRE AND SABRE SIX SPECIFICATIONS

	Sabre	**Sabre Six**
Layout and chassis	Fabricated steel box-section chassis with glass-fibre body and bonded-in plywood floors. Coupé or open-topped with optional hard top	Fabricated steel box-section chassis with glass-fibre body and bonded-in plywood floors. Coupé or open-topped with optional hard top
Engine	Ford Consul 375	Ford Zephyr 6
Type	4-cylinder in line	6-cylinder in line
Block material	Cast iron	Cast iron
Head material	Cast iron	Cast iron
Cylinders	4	6
Cooling	Pressurized water and antifreeze mix	Pressurized water and antifreeze mix
Bore and stroke	82.6 x 79.5mm	82.6 x 79.5mm
Capacity	1703cc	2553cc
Valves	Two per cylinder	Two per cylinder
Compression ratio	7.8:1	8.3:1
Carburettor	Single Zenith downdraught	Single Zenith downdraught
Max power (claimed)	59bhp @ 4,400rpm	109bhp @ 4,800rpm
Max torque	91lb/ft @ 2,300rpm	137lb/ft @ 2,400rpm
Fuel capacity	8.25 gallons/37.5 litres	12 gallons/54.5 litres
Transmission		
Gearbox	ZF four-speed with optional overdrive	Ford four-speed with optional overdrive
Clutch	Single plate, diaphragm spring	Single plate, diaphragm spring
Ratios		
1st	2.53:1	3.16 (o/d 2.43):1
2nd	1.69:1	2.21 (o/d 1.70):1
3rd	1.23:1	1.41 (o/d 1.19):1
4th	1:1	1.0 (o/d 0.77):1
Reverse	2.59:1	3.34:1
Final drive	3.55:1	3.58:1

As Reliant developed the Sabre, it became more mainstream, especially in the suspension department. Fitted with the Ford 6-cylinder engine, the Sabre Six was a good, typically British sports car with a respectable performance and rugged, reliable mechanics, but it always struggled to generate sales against the competition – the UK's established sports-car manufacturers. The experience Reliant gained in the design, development and production of the Sabre proved invaluable, however, when the company moved from the pure sports-car market, as epitomized by the Sabre, into the more mature GT-car market, with the Scimitar.

The Sabre was produced between 1961 and 1964, in two versions: the 4-cylinder Sabre Four SE1 (1961–1963), of which forty-four were built, and the 6-cylinder Sabre Six SE2 (1962–1964), of which seventy-seven were produced, giving a total of 121 cars. In addition to these, Reliant produced a single Sabra/Sabre prototype, and 162 left-hand-drive Sabras, while Autocars produced 171 more left-hand-drive Sabras, giving a grand total of 334 Sabras.

	Sabre	Sabre Six
Suspension and steering		
Suspension front	Leading-arm, coil over damper	Initially leading-arm, coil over damper, replaced by Triumph-based independent double wishbone, coil springs and damper, anti-roll bar
Suspension rear	Live rear axle, fore and aft locating arms and Watts linkage. Coil over dampers	Live rear axle, fore and aft locating arms and Watts linkage. Coil over dampers
Steering	Rack and pinion	Rack and pinion
Tyres	155x15 radial	165x15 radial
Wheels	4.25in width steel or knock-on wire wheels	4.25in width steel or knock-on wire wheels
Brakes		
Type	Disc front, drum rear	Disc front, drum rear
Size: front	10.5in diameter	10.4in diameter
Size: rear	9in diameter x 1.75in width	9in diameter x 1.5in width
Dimensions		
Track: front	51in/129cm	48in/122cm
Track: rear	50in/127cm	48in/122cm
Wheelbase	90in/228.6cm	90in/228.6cm
Overall length	165in/419cm	160in/406.4cm
Overall width	61in/155cm	61in/155cm
Overall height	50in/127cm	51in/129.5cm
Kerb weight	1,827lb/828.7kg	2,219lb/1,006.5kg
Performance		
Top speed	90mph/145km/h	118mph/190km/h
0–60mph	16 secs	12 secs

CHAPTER 3

INTO THE GT MARKET:
THE SCIMITAR GT (1965–1969)

INTRODUCTION

While the Sabre Six, with its revised suspension and decent performance, was a reasonable sports car, by the mid-1960s the bodywork was starting to look dated, and the stigma of its 1950s kit-car ancestry was a negative influence on potential customers. Along with these issues, the car's relatively small size, cramped interior and overtly sporting characteristics resulted in a vehicle that was raw and visceral but not particularly comfortable, which meant that its appeal was somewhat limited to the hard core end of the sports-car market.

Reliant's management, in the form of Ray Wiggen, realized that, if Reliant was to continue building sports cars, the only way forward was to move into a market with the potential for a significant increase in sales and higher profit margins on the product. This market was essentially the GT sector, which would be attractive to Reliant's existing Sabre customers as they matured, and would also attract new buyers who wanted a stylish, attractive GT car for serious touring, but who could not afford an Aston Martin, a Bentley or a Bristol. In order to enter this market Reliant would have to design a car with additional space and accessibility for passengers in both the front and rear seats, and adequate space for luggage. Along with the extra space, the GT class demanded greater levels of comfort and refinement than the Sabre offered, in order to address the motoring needs of enthusiasts with family responsibilities.

The catalyst for the new Reliant GT car was the Ogle SX250, a bang up-to-date design for a stylish glass-fibre-bodied two-door coupé, shown at the October 1962 London Motor Show at Earls Court. The SX250 was Ogle Design's third car, following its Riley-based 1.5 and Mini-based SX1000, and was in essence a rebodied Daimler SP250 sports car with room for two adults up front and two children (or one adult) in the rear. At the time, as well as looking to update or replace the Sabre, Reliant was starting to design its first economy-market four-wheeler, the diminutive Rebel. Seeing the SX250, Reliant's Ray Wiggen realized that, while the SX250 design was not for sale at the time, Ogle could be a useful design resource. He commissioned Ogle to style the car that would become the Rebel, instigating a long and fruitful relationship for both companies. After the motor show, once Ogle had started to style the new Reliant Rebel, the SX250 design also became available, and Reliant bought the rights to it.

OPPOSITE PAGE:
TOP: **The Scimitar had all-new bodywork that was designed by Ogle and fitted to a modified Sabre chassis, to give Reliant an all-new GT car.**

BOTTOM: **The Scimitar's design was sleek and modern and made a fine long-distance GT car. This early model is pictured at the RSSOC 2017 sprint at Curborough.**

OGLE DESIGN AND THE RELIANT CONNECTION

The well-respected British-based and -owned design agency David Ogle Associates was set up in 1954 by David Ogle. Having carried out design briefs for various clients and produced a number of industrial design classics, such as the iconic Bush TR82 portable radio, by 1959 the company had grown to four designers and one secretary. They decided to take on the Italian coachbuilders and stylists by entering the transport arena, becoming the only British-owned design bureau in this important market. Ogle's first foray into car design, the Ogle 1.5, was a sleek two-door coupé based on the Riley 1.5 saloon. Although the car was well received by the press of the day, only eight were produced. In 1960, a subsidiary company, David Ogle Ltd, was set up to make cars designed by David Ogle Associates.

The 1.5 was followed in 1962 by the SX1000, which was based on the BMC Mini and followed the same method of construction as the Ogle 1.5, with a highly modified Mini monocoque mated to a glass-fibre two-door coupé body. The SX1000 was a quick and quirky take on the Mini, and about sixty-six examples were made between 1962 and 1964.

After the tragic death of founder David Ogle in 1962, in a road traffic accident in his SX1000, John Ogier took over as chairman, and Tom Karen, who had worked for the company in its early days but had moved to Murphy, rejoined as Chief Designer. The Ogle SX1000 was launched alongside the Ogle SX250 at the 1962 Motor Show. The SX250 was the third example of Ogle's car design skills – a rebodied Daimler SP250 with a two-door 2+2 coupé-style body sitting on the Daimler's chassis and running gear. It had been privately commissioned from Ogle by Boris Fortner, one of the directors of the cosmetics company Helena Rubenstein. Originally, Fortner had wanted to make a run of six cars for sale to his friends, but in the event only two cars were completed. The design was also offered to Daimler as an SP250 replacement but, with Daimler soon to be bought by Jaguar, this route was also to prove fruitless.

After seeing Ogle's SX1000 and SX250 at the 1962 Earls Court Motor Show, Reliant commissioned the agency to style the Rebel, Reliant's first small four-wheeler for the domestic market. Although the SX250 design was not for sale at the time of the show, after Fortner's project stalled and Daimler showed no interest, it did become available and Reliant was able to buy it and use it to form the basis of the Reliant Scimitar Coupé. The collaboration would lead, via the Triplex GTS, to the 1968 Scimitar GTE.

LEFT: **Ogle's SX1000 was based on the Mini and made a fine small GT car.**

RIGHT: **The Ogle Triplex GTS was designed for the Triplex glass company as a technology demonstrator. It was later used by the Duke of Edinburgh as his personal car.**
DAVE POOLE

The SX250, based on the Daimler SP250, was designed by Ogle for Boris Fortner, the head of the Helena Rubenstein cosmetics company, and formed the basis for the Scimitar GT. The main styling change raised the height of the waist-level styling line. RACEBEARS UK

The Ogle Triplex GTS ('Glazing Test Special') was a development of the Scimitar Coupé, carried out by Ogle on behalf of Triplex to demonstrate the advances made in automotive glass. While it kept the Scimitar's wheelbase, it was a two-box design, keeping the Scimitar's nose but with an estate-type passenger cell extending the length of the car. The car featured extensive glazing, to show Triplex's various types of glass, including a heated rear window, 'Syndyne' heat-absorbing glass on the roof and laminated safety glass. It also demonstrated the use of bonding techniques to attach the various glass panels to the car. The car was later used by the Duke of Edinburgh for a while as his personal vehicle, leading to a long association between Reliant and Princess Anne, who owned a succession of GTEs. While the GTS was a one-off, it did indirectly lead to Reliant's most famous sports car, the GTE, which was also designed by Ogle.

Ogle's designers continued to work with Reliant to style its sports, saloon and utility cars, including the Bond Bug and Robin, until the late 1970s and the arrival of the SS1, which was styled by the Italian coachbuilder Giovanni Michelotti.

SCIMITAR GT SE4

Design and Development

With the basis of the SX250, Reliant had an up-to-date and stylish body, which needed only to be adapted to the existing well-proven Sabre Six chassis to produce a viable production car. The integration process was not as straightforward as it looked, however. The dimensions of the Sabre and Daimler chassis were different, with an extra 2 inches (5cm) in the wheelbase of the Daimler, the Reliant's rear track was 1.5 inches (3.75cm) wider, and there were significant internal issues with the new body shell. While the SX250 body shell was constructed mainly from glass fibre, the Ogle design incorporated steel inserts in the door hinge plates, which were supported by tubes running forwards to the chassis. It also had a sheet-steel bulkhead and, at the rear, a second double-skinned transverse 'A'-shaped steel bulkhead, sited between the rear seat rest and the luggage boot. The door shuts were steel, and additional channel section risers were fitted to the tops of the rear frame to enable the spare wheel to be housed below the level of the boot floor. Finally, the rear seats were far too small to be practical, and the doors were too short to afford easy access to the rear seats. All these issues had to be addressed before the car could be put into production.

Chassis

The SX250's Daimler SP250 chassis was originally based on the Triumph TR3 unit, as was the front suspension, which in turn was derived from the Triumph Mayflower. It was made for Triumph by Alford and Alder and was very similar to the front suspension already in use on the Sabre Six. Using the Daimler chassis would have had licensing implications, so Reliant decided to press ahead with a development of the Sabre Six chassis, which retained the Triumph-derived front suspension and multi-link rear-axle location. The main change needed was to the wheelbase, with an additional 2.5 inches (6.25cm) inserted into the middle of the chassis to fit Reliant's rework of the Ogle body.

Body and Interior

While the Scimitar retained the style and overall shape of the Ogle design, the body shell was extensively reworked, both to fit on the modified Sabre Six chassis and to make it suitable for mass production. The most significant change from the Ogle design was the complete re-engineering of the body, to remove the sheet-steel rear bulkhead, and the modification of the front-bulkhead steel reinforcements. The result was a strong and rigid all-glass-fibre moulding with some steel reinforcement.

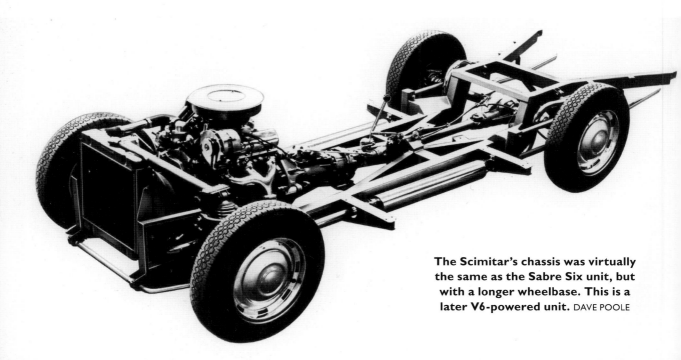

The Scimitar's chassis was virtually the same as the Sabre Six unit, but with a longer wheelbase. This is a later V6-powered unit. DAVE POOLE

The Scimitar's glass-fibre body shell was moulded in three main parts: the outer shell, an inner lining that combined the floor and scuttle, and an engine bay lining. These internal mouldings gave the shell structural integrity and strength, and also provided a much better internal finish than on the Sabre. The gel coating on the interior sides reduced the amount of exposed matt (the rough side of the glass fibre) in the cabin and the engine bay. The door sills were reinforced with 'Z'-section steel beams, and further steel reinforcements were used to form a cage around the passenger compartment. Vertical steel pillars were welded to the front of the sill members, to reinforce the 'A' pillar and provide strong mounts for the door hinges. From the scuttle level, tubular steel loops ran up the screen pillar, over the door top and back down behind the rear side window to the waistline, and were welded to the top of a 'U'-section steel insert in each 'B' pillar.

A bracing tube ran across the car's roof at the top of the windscreen and was joined to the 'A' pillar reinforcement to join both sides of the structure

ABOVE: **While the Scimitar's body shell was mainly glass fibre, there was steel reinforcement bonded in place. Visible here underneath the glass fibre is the steel reinforcement above the rear window.**

BELOW: **The original Scimitar had a Ford straight-six engine. It was fitted quite far back in the chassis to give decent weight distribution.**

together. Steel plates were positioned in the door-shut area of the 'B' pillar, to reinforce the door lock latches, but were not connected to the reinforcement above the car's waistline. The various steel members were permanently bonded into the body shell and formed a rigid cage around the passenger cell, as well as adding significant stiffness to the body. As on the Sabre, the complete body shell was bolted to the chassis. The doors had no steel reinforcement, but the structures were stiffened using deep ribbing on the inside of the panels and the doors were lengthened, to give better access to the interior. A metal frame carried the glass, and the top of this was angled inwards towards the roof, giving space to incorporate pockets into the inside edge of the doors, while leaving enough room for the widow-winding mechanism.

Opening quarter-lights were fitted at the front edge of the glass frame in the doors. The rear side windows were hinged on their front edge and could be opened to act as extractor vents to increase airflow through the car. The styling retained the overall lines of the SX250, but, where the SX250 had a pronounced cheat line down its flanks, which flattened the top of its rear wheel arches, the Scimitar had more rounded rear wheel arches that sat below the styling line that ran around the front of the front wheel arch, along the side of the body and terminated at the tail of the car. A Wilmot Breedon sliding sunroof – either manual or electrically operated – could be specified as an extra. At the front of the car a pair of 5.5-inch (14-cm) diameter headlights were recessed in oval pods on each side; below them, just above the chromed front bumper, sat a combined indicator and parking light. On each side of the rear panel, above the rear bumper, were a pair of round lights – a red one for rear marker and brakes, and an amber one for indicators. A small rectangular reflector

The original press car, BUE 441B, has been restored and appears at many shows. This interior shot shows the dash and centre console.

sat below each pair of lights and there was a pair of round reversing lights under the bumper.

The rear-hinged bonnet sat flush on the front deck and opened reasonably widely, with a mechanical strut to support it. Under the bonnet, the inner liner meant that the engine bay surfaces were all smooth gel-coating, making them easy to clean. One notable point was the positioning of the two 6-volt batteries on the front corners of the engine bay on each side of the radiator.

At the rear, the boot lid wrapped around the rear wings and tail, to ensure good weatherproofing and easy draining of water away from the opening. In the boot, the spare wheel sat horizontally in a well, and was covered by a lift-out glass-fibre panel, which had recesses moulded into its top face to carry the tools and the jack. With the panel in place, the boot floor was flat and provided a wide and deep luggage area.

Reliant was very pleased with the end result of the design process, which was a coupé with plenty of room for the front-seat passengers, as well as space for either two children or a single adult in the rear.

ABOVE: **The boot floor of the Scimitar was formed from a neat spare-wheel cover with moulded-in tool storage.**

BELOW: **The first Scimitar, the GT, had wire wheels. Note the styling line on the waist, which runs above the rear wheel arch.**

Engine, Gearbox and Final Drive

When it was launched, the Scimitar GT was fitted with the Ford Zephyr straight-six unit from the Sabre Six. The engine had a cast-iron block and cylinder head, and a bore and stroke of 82.6 x 79.5mm, giving a capacity of 2553cc. In the Scimitar application it was lightly tuned, to give the car an acceptable performance. With an 8.3:1 compression ratio and three SU carburettors, the power output was 120bhp at 5,000rpm along with 140lb/ft of torque at 2,600rpm.

The car came with a standard Ford four-speed (and reverse) gearbox that had originally been fitted to the straight-six-engined Zephyr and Zodiac saloons. This had synchromesh on the forward ratios and could also be fitted with an electrically operated Type 230 Auto Transmissions De Normanville overdrive unit with a drive ratio of 0.82. A four-speed ZF gearbox as used on the Sabre was also listed as an option, but it is unclear if any were actually fitted. The live rear axle from the Sabre was retained.

At least one and possibly two development Scimitars were equipped with a Ford automatic gearbox by the factory in the early days of Scimitar production. However, the auto box was not offered to the public as an option.

Suspension

As a modified Sabre chassis formed the basis of the new Scimitar, the Sabre Six's front and rear suspension layout, with its independent front and dual link rear system featuring the fore and aft Ballamy-Reliant linkage, was carried over on to the new car. However, the Scimitar was not intended to be an out-and-out sports car like the Sabre, but a GT car, which had to be capable of covering long distances in comfort and safety. Reliant needed to ensure a comfortable ride combined with good handling and road-holding, so the Sabre's stiffness and harsh ride had to be tuned out. A significant amount of research into spring rates for the front and rear suspension of the new car resulted in significantly softer springs being specified, along with Aeon rubber doughnuts being fitted into the damper rods, to act as progressive bump stops when the suspension approached full upward travel. Rear axle vertical movement was limited by the fitting of webbing straps to limit downward movement of the rear axle and wheels.

Despite the development work put into the rear suspension, the Scimitar still displayed some of the unwelcome handling characteristics that had been seen on the Sabre. Although it was not considered to be dangerous, the rear axle's location was questionable.

The first straight-six-powered Scimitars had triple SU carbs and a pair of batteries, one on each side of the radiator. The smooth gel-coated interior surfaces made the engine bay tidy and easy to clean.

**The first Scimitar's interior, with its plain flat wooden dashboard with
a simple centre console and two-tone seats, was a bit of a departure
from that of the Sabre, with its sculpted instrument binnacle.**

It could lead to the axle shifting when going into a corner, which would initially unsettle the car (and driver), although the car would then settle down and follow a more predictable path.

Brakes and Wheels

The Scimitar was equipped with disc brakes on the front and drums on the rear, the de facto set-up for sporting cars of the 1960s. Initially, the set-up was the same as on the Sabre, with 10.6-inch diameter solid discs and Girling two-piston calipers. After the first fifty cars had been completed, the fronts were upgraded, with new Girling calipers with three cylinders – a large-diameter one on the inside and two smaller-diameter ones on the outside – to upgrade the braking from the Sabre. The Scimitar's calipers were shared with the Jaguar 420G, a heavier and higher-performance car, and Reliant's car's brakes benefited greatly from the fitment.

As standard, the Scimitar came with 15-inch diameter seventy-two-spoke centre-lock wire wheels in 5J rim width in contrast to the Sabre Six's weaker sixty-spoke items. The 165x15 Pirelli Cinturato radial tyres that were fitted as standard were quite a rarity at the time, when crossply tyres were still in vogue.

SCIMITAR DEVELOPMENT

Over the lifetime of the Scimitar, Reliant made a number of changes to the car, resulting in the SE4a, SE4b and SE4c. The first 297 SE4 cars used the Ford straight-six 2553cc engine. After that, with the introduction of the SE4a, the Ford Essex 3-litre V6 unit was used, and the rear suspension was modified to incorporate twin trailing arms and a Watts linkage. The SE4b was a lightly updated SE4a, with an improved interior. The final model, the SE4c, was an 'economy' model powered by the 2.5-litre version of the Essex V6, introduced alongside the SE4b after the fuel crisis of 1967.

Scimitar 3-Litre SE4a

The Scimitar SE4a replaced the SE4 model and was launched at the London Earls Court Motor Show in October 1966 for the 1967 model year. The main motivation for the change was the fact that Ford had replaced the Consul-based straight-six engine with the 3-litre Essex V6 unit, so the new Scimitar adopted the new engine. The Essex V6 unit was the same as that used in the Ford Zodiac, with a bore and stroke of 93.7 × 72.42mm, giving a capacity of 2994cc. When fitted with the standard Ford issue Weber 40DFA-1 carburettor, it had a power output of 144bhp at 4,500rpm and torque of 192.5lb/ft at 3,000rpm. In the SE4a, the V6 unit was kept in standard tune by Reliant, to ensure the validity of the Ford warranty. At the launch of the new car, the company claimed a 0–60 time of 10 seconds and a top speed in excess of 125mph (200km/h), representing a small but significant performance jump from the GT's 0–60 in 11.5 seconds and 117mph (188km/h) top speed. The V6 unit was significantly shorter than the outgoing straight-six, and as such sat further back in the chassis; this helped to reduce the weight on the front end, but also had the disadvantage of limiting access to the engine.

In addition to a new engine, the SE4a also had significant revisions made to its suspension. The SE4's handling had been found in practice to be sensitive under hard cornering, so John Crosthwaite, a former BRM chassis designer, was brought in by Reliant to have a look at it. As a result, the front suspension wishbone mounts on the chassis were lowered, to reduce the roll centre of the car; the front suspension towers were strengthened; an additional crossmember was fitted at the front of the chassis; and an anti-roll bar was fitted to the front suspension for the first time. At the rear, the original Scimitar's fore and aft angled Ballamy-Reliant links were replaced by a pair of trailing arms on each side, which were mounted parallel to the centre line of the car to control the up and down movement of the axle properly. A transverse Watts link was added to locate the axle transversely. This system no longer relied on the compliance of the rubber mounts to control axle movement and the system gave a much better set of handling characteristics, as the springs and dampers could actually do their job in controlling the vertical movement. The modifications also increased the rear-wheel movement by 3 inches (about 7.5cm), which, as it

The engine bay on the later V6 Scimitars was a lot 'busier' than the bay on the straight-six versions. This is Geoff Richards' SE4c, which has a number of non-standard fittings, including electrics and cooling-system modifications.

LEFT: **The later (SE4b) Scimitar had a revised interior, with air vents at each end of the dash and a hooded main dash to cut down reflections.**

BELOW: **The Scimitar's rear seats were strictly for children only, or a single adult could sit sideways.**

was properly controlled by the coil over damper units, aided both cornering ability and comfort. Axle movement was controlled by the dampers, and the webbing straps used on the earlier cars were discarded.

The wire wheels were replaced by bolt-on 15-inch diameter steel wheels with eight small holes in the outer edge of the disc and small chrome hub caps covering the wheel nuts. Tyres were still Pirelli Cinturato radials, but the size was now 165x15. Evidence shows that some of last straight-six-powered SE4s produced were fitted with the revised suspension before the introduction of the V6-powered SE4a. The ZF gearbox option was formally discontinued and a standard Ford Zodiac four-speed unit was fitted, with the option of an overdrive.

New body features included redesigned and strengthened door pillars and hinges and a collapsible steering column with two universal joints. Interior mouldings were altered to provide the ducting for a new fresh-air system, with two eyeball vents positioned at each of the dashboard. A new hooded dashboard moulding was covered in black vinyl rather than wood. Reliant made great play of the fact that this new dashboard increased safety, as it cut down reflections in the instrument faces. The instruments were also fitted with matt black rather than chrome bezels, again to reduce reflections, and the face-level eyeball-type vents and the facia were also in 'anti-dazzle' black. An optional heated rear screen was also offered. Reshaped rear-seat backrests gave

slightly more room to the rear-seat passengers and the seats gained basketweave-patterned vinyl on the centre sections, to add some texture to the interior.

Scimitar 3-Litre SE4b

Introduced alongside the SE4c (see below), the SE4b featured just a light cosmetic update to the interior, and retained the 3-litre V6 and mechanicals of the SE4a.

RELIANT EXPERIENCES

GEOFF RICHARDS' SCIMITAR SE4B

Geoff Richards has owned his Scimitar Coupé for over twenty years and in that time he has built the car into an accomplished long-distance tourer, which has taken him in comfort all over the UK and into Europe. With its classic yellow paintwork, done over twenty-five years ago and still looking good, the car had been restored before Geoff bought it. Since then, he has refined and tweaked the car to improve both its practicality and performance, while keeping all the improvements reversible for the purists.

The car's interior is lovely. Geoff has retained all of the period charm of Reliant's original set-up, but has enhanced the cabin ambiance with a walnut dashboard that adds an air of luxury. Another improvement is the extractor vent fitted to the rear wing on the driver's side; positioned in a low-pressure area, this helps achieve a decent airflow through the car by extracting stale air from the cabin.

THIS PAGE:
Geoff Richards has owned his Scimitar Coupé (SE4b) for over twenty years. He uses it for long-distance work and it is a fine example of the breed.

OPPOSITE PAGE:
TOP: **The Scimitar's sleek lines suit the use of bright colours.**

BOTTOM: **From the rear quarter, Geoff Richards' Scimitar shows its rear panel and athletic stance.**

(continued overleaf)

GEOFF RICHARDS' SCIMITAR SE4B

Probably the best 'GT' modification is the changing of the Laycock De Normanville's overdrive ratio, to give a higher 'step up' (from the standard 0.82:1 to 0.76:1). At the UK legal motorway limit of 70mph, the engine in overdrive top turns over at a mere 2,300rpm, sitting nicely in the middle of the engine's power and torque curves and still affording instant acceleration when required. An added bonus is the surprisingly low level of noise at these speeds, which allows the driver and passenger to have a normal conversation and listen to the radio, just like in a modern car. This all helps to make the car ideally suited to fast long-distance travelling – of course, that is what the Scimitar is all about!

Elsewhere in the car, the main modifications are evident in the ancillary systems – cooling, fuel supply and electrics. The cooling has been extensively reworked, with an electric water pump replacing the original mechanical unit and revised flow paths, to ensure that both heads get a decent flow of coolant through them. This is something that the original system was not good at achieving. The electric pump also helps to cut down heat-soak issues – it runs on for about two minutes after the engine has been turned off, to continue the cooling down of the unit. The fuel is now supplied to the Weber carburettor via a pair of electric pumps with a pressure limiting valve and a recirculation function, which ensures a good supply of fresh petrol to the carb and helps to avoid the vaporization issues from which modern fuels seem to suffer. Finally, with an uprated alternator, relays to control most circuits, properly fused circuits and a single large-capacity battery replacing the two smaller units fitted as standard, the car's electrical system is reliable and can handle the additional demands from the extra components.

The subtly flared rear wheel arches accommodate 6J x 15-inch alloy wheels, as fitted to the Middlebridge GTE, with 195/65 x 15 tyres; they give Geoff both slightly higher gearing and a better choice of modern rubber than the original 5.5J x 15-inch steel wheels that were fitted with 165x15 tyres (Pirelli Cinturato). The brakes are also uprated front and rear. At the front, new Wilwood calipers grip ventilated discs, while at the rear the original Salisbury 7HA axle drums have been uprated to GTE specification and a limiting valve has been fitted, to avoid lock-ups. The differential has been converted to a limited slip unit with a ratio of 3.31:1 (original ratio 3.58:1), again raising the gearing from standard. The suspension has been treated with adjustable spring platform shock absorbers and Geoff has spent some time tuning the ride height front and rear to cure a disturbing front end, which became light and vague at high speed. This has been cured by dropping the front ride height a couple of inches and raising the rear by about an inch using the adjustment. This has given the car a neutral, positive feel all the way up to its top speed of around 120/125mph (192/200km/h).

All in all, Geoff's SE4a is an excellent example of a classic that has been sensibly and sensitively upgraded to meet the demands of today's busy roads and its owner's particular needs.

Scimitar 2.5-Litre SE4c

Introduced in August 1967, in a climate of increasing oil prices and the threat of petrol rationing in the UK as a result of the Arab-Israeli Six Days' War in June 1967, the SE4c was identical to the then current SE4a, except that it was fitted with a 2.5-litre Essex V6 – and a new badge on the rear, indicating the changed engine size. The 3-litre model's standard radial ply Pirelli Cinturato tyres became an option, although the SE4c retained the same-sized wheels. The engine was a short-stroke version of the Ford's 3-litre Zephyr unit, usually seen in the Ford Zodiac 6, and had a bore and stroke of 93.67 x 60.35mm, giving a true capacity of 2495cc, and a power output of 119bhp at 4,750rpm and torque of 146lb/ft at 3,000rpm. The 2.5-litre engine was fitted with a Zenith carburettor rather than the 3-litre's Weber, and it retained the larger engine's external dimensions, making it a straightforward replacement for the SE4a's 3-litre unit. The aim of the Scimitar SE4c was to widen the appeal of the car, with better fuel consumption, albeit accompanied by a slight drop in performance. It was priced at £1,395 (including purchase tax), offering a significant saving of £121 over the price of the SE4b Scimitar 3-litre. The smaller engine would also drop the car into cheaper tax classes in some European countries.

In August 1968, the TR4-derived front suspension that had been used since the introduction of the Scimitar was replaced on the SE4b and SE4c by a TR6-based set-up. While this retained the twin-wishbone layout, it had new, stronger vertical links, and replaced the brass bushes in the lower wishbone outer ends by maintenance-free nylon 'top hat' items. The change also required a modification in the design of the steel wheels, to give adequate clearance for the new suspension components.

SCIMITAR SUMMARY

The Scimitar GT moved Reliant from its position as a manufacturer of low-volume, raw and quirky sports cars, such as the Sabre, to a mainstream supplier of upmarket GT cars. With its up-to-date styling, long range and a great combination of performance and practicality, the Scimitar was much more successful and sold in greater numbers than the Sabre. One aspect of the Scimitar is the ease of entry and exit – I for one can attest to the fact that it is a lot easier for a six-foot four-inch adult of a certain age to get in and out of a Scimitar than a Sabre!

The Scimitar Coupe was announced in 1964, with deliveries starting in 1965 and production ending in 1970. There were four versions: the SE4 (1965–1966), of which 297 were built; the SE4a (1966–1968), of which 539 were produced; the SE4b (1967–1970), of which fifty-one were built; and the SE4c (1967–1970), of which 118 were produced, giving a grand total of 1,005 cars.

On the road the Scimitar looks every inch the classic it is.

SCIMITAR SPECIFICATIONS

	Scimitar GT	**Scimitar SE4b**	**Scimitar SE4c**
Layout and chassis	2+2 Coupé. Fabricated steel box-section chassis with glass-fibre body	2+2 Coupé. Fabricated steel box-section chassis with glass-fibre body	2+2 Coupé. Fabricated steelbox-section chassis with glass-fibre body
Engine	Ford Zephyr 6	Ford Essex 3-litre	Ford Essex 2.5-litre
Type	6-cylinder in line	V6	V6
Block material	Cast iron	Cast iron	Cast iron
Head material	Cast iron	Cast iron	Cast iron
Cylinders	6	6	6
Cooling	Pressurized water and antifreeze mix	Pressurized water and antifreeze mix	Pressurized water and antifreeze mix
Bore and stroke	82.6 x 79.5mm	93.67 x 72.42mm	93.67 x 60.35mm
Capacity	2553cc	2994cc	2495cc
Valves	Two per cylinder	Two per cylinder	Two per cylinder
Compression ratio	8.3:1	8.9:1	9.1:1
Carburettor	3 x SU HS4	Twin-choke Weber 40DFA-1	Zenith 38.1 VT downdraught
Max power (claimed)	120bhp @ 5,000rpm	128bhp @ 4,500rpm	119bhp @ 4,750rpm
Max torque	140lb/ft @ 2,600rpm	176lb/ft @ 3,000rpm	146lb/ft @ 3,000rpm
Fuel capacity	20 gallons/91 litres	21 gallons/95.5 litres	21 gallons/95.5 litres
Transmission			
Gearbox	Ford four-speed with overdrive on 3rd and 4th (0.82:1)	Ford four-speed with overdrive on 3rd and 4th (0.82:1)	Ford four-speed with overdrive on 3rd and 4th (0.82:1)
Clutch	Single plate, diaphragm spring	Single plate, diaphragm spring	Single plate, diaphragm spring
Ratios			
1st	3.16:1	3.16:1	3.16:1
2nd	2.21:1	2.21:1	2.21:1
3rd	1.4 (o/d 1.1):1	1.4 (o/d 1.1):1	1.4 (o/d 1.1):1
4th	1.0 (o/d 0.778):1	1.0 (o/d 0.778):1	1.0 (o/d 0.778):1
Reverse	3.35:1	3.33:1	3.33:1
Final drive	3.88:1	3.58:1	3.58:1

	Scimitar GT	Scimitar SE4b	Scimitar SE4c
Suspension and steering			
Suspension front	Triumph-based independent double wishbone, coil springs and damper	Triumph-based independent double wishbone, coil springs and damper, anti-roll bar	Triumph-based independent double wishbone, coil springs and damper, anti-roll bar
Suspension rear	Live rear axle, fore and aft locating arms and Watts linkage. Coil over dampers	Live rear axle, twin trailing arms and Watts linkage. Coil over dampers	Live rear axle, twin trailing arms and Watts linkage. Coil over dampers
Steering	Rack and pinion	Rack and pinion	Rack and pinion
Tyres	165x15 radial	165x15 radial	165x15 radial
Wheels	15-in centre-lock wire wheels	5.5J x 15in pressed steel	5.5J x 15in pressed steel
Rim width	–	–	–
Brakes			
Type	Disc front, drum rear	Disc front, drum rear	Disc front, drum rear
Size: front	10.6in diameter	10.6in diameter	10.6in diameter
Size: rear	9in diameter x 1.75in width	9in diameter x 1.75in width	9in diameter x 1.75in width
Dimensions			
Track: front	50in/127cm	51.5in/131cm	51.5in/131cm
Track: rear	50in/127cm	50.5in/128cm	50.5in/128cm
Wheelbase	92.5in/235cm	92.5in/235cm	92.5in/235cm
Overall length	167in/424.2cm	167in/424.2cm	167in/424.2cm
Overall width	64in/162.6cm	64in/162.6cm	64in/162.6cm
Overall height	51.5in/130.8cm	51.5in/130.8cm	51.5in/130.8cm
Kerb weight	2,414 lb/1,095 kg	2,419.2 lb/1,097 kg	2,419.2 lb/1,097 kg
Performance			
Top speed	117mph/188.3km/h	119.3mph/192km/h	114mph/184km/h
0–60mph	11 secs	9.4 secs	10.5 secs

CHAPTER 4

THE FIRST SPORTS ESTATE:
THE SCIMITAR GTE SE5 (1968–1975)

INTRODUCTION

When the Scimitar GTE was announced to the press, in August 1968, and exhibited at that month's London Earls Court Motor Show, it marked the start of a successful couple of decades for the Reliant GT car range. Building on the company's experience of making an upmarket coupé with the Scimitar, and with Ogle's innovative, practical and attractive design, the GTE addressed a market niche that no other manufacturer had identified, let alone satisfied. At the time of the GTE's introduction, the sports-car market was rather limited: first, there was the small, sporting car that appealed to the young, free and

The GTE was Reliant's most successful sports car. The distinctive rear end, with its rising rear waistline, avoided the 'bread van' look of other estate cars.

The 'Three-Litre Scimitar by Ogle' was Ogle's own take on the GTE theme, with a glass roof and Ogle logo moulded into the front wings, as well as shutters to conceal the headlights. Only one was made.
DAVE POOLE

single character; and, second, the sports coupé, which gave the slightly more mature and potentially married customer a GT car that could be used for more serious travel in some comfort, without sacrificing performance. After these two stages of an owner-driver's life, the customer who wanted more practicality and room in a car would be looking at a four-door saloon or estate, and would probably forego the delights of a sports model. The GTE changed this overnight. With its ability to seat four adults comfortably, and a three-door estate format, it offered the holy grail of the sports-car market – a sporting GT car that was also practical. With the car's unique practicality, combined with the bonus of its brilliant Ogle style, with the upswept rear waistline that avoided the uninspiring van-like appearance of most existing estate cars, it was obvious that Reliant had a success on their hands.

Alongside Reliant's GTE, Ogle Design also exhibited its take on the GTE theme at Earls Court. Called the 'Three-Litre Scimitar by Ogle', the car retained the Reliant's basic outline and dimensions, but incorporated a number of design features not used on Reliant's GTE. These included the use of a glass panel over the front seats, as first seen on the Triplex GTS, and Ogle logos embossed into the moulding on the front wings. The front end was reworked and featured four new Lucas rectangular sealed beam 60-watt head lamps, which were covered when not in use by electrically operated shutters, giving the nose a clean and uncluttered look. The interior also came in for a

modernist makeover, with a light tan leather trim and chequered fabric on the seat facings. The alterations did not make production, however, although later GTEs did have tan trim, and the only example was sold to the Chairman of Reliant, Sir Julian Hodge. This unique car is still owned by the Hodge family.

DESIGN AND DEVELOPMENT

When Reliant's GTE was launched, in October 1968, it received unanimous acclaim from the motoring press. The general view was that its clever seating and luggage arrangements made the car truly unique and versatile. The GTE's first brochure emphasized the difference:

> Only Reliant offer the benefits of a grand tourer and a capacious estate in one car able to take four adult passengers and their luggage for long distances, at high speeds, in extreme comfort. Reliant are the first manufacturer to put such a vehicle into production.

The GTE's existence can be traced back to the Ogle/Triplex GTS, which was produced in 1965. With its versatile load space, adequate seating for two or possibly three, and sporting performance, the one-off GTS took the first steps in identifying a completely new market sector. The Reliant Scimitar GTE was the car that would come to define that sector – offering

The versatile rear load space of the GTE was one of its unique selling points. Even with both of the folding rear seats up, there was an impressive luggage space of 19 cubic feet available; with one seat down (as shown here), it was 27 cubic feet.

the first true four-seat estate GT – and would provide the class leader for the following two decades.

Building on its experience of building a successful GT car, in the shape of the Scimitar Coupé, Reliant carried the mechanical strengths of the Scimitar forwards, while redefining the bodywork and chassis to provide a new design with no compromises. The design had to be practical, providing accommodation for four adult passengers as well as decent and flexible load-carrying capacity, and it also had to look both sporting and attractive. Ogle's body design, combined with an all-new chassis, which was wider and longer than the Scimitar Coupé's unit, resulted in a car that could accommodate four adults in relative comfort along with a versatile luggage area.

Chassis

The GTE's chassis was an all-new unit, but had the same layout for the front and rear suspension as on the Scimitar Coupé. In order to give four adult passengers and their luggage adequate room, the new chassis had to be long enough to accommodate full-size rear seats and the luggage platform, and wider than the existing Scimitar unit, in order to allow for reasonably sized footwells for both the front and rear passengers. The original Scimitar GT's chassis was too short to allow for rear seats of a reasonable size, and its parallel side members meant that the space needed for the footwells was already filled with ironwork.

The GTE's chassis was laid out with the main fore and aft chassis members in a cruciform or 'X'-shaped form, with the two main longitudinal rails squeezed together within the wheelbase. On each side of the chassis were outriggers to support the outer edges of the body between the wheels and provide some crash protection to the car's occupants.

The design enabled the seats to be positioned between the centre chassis members and the outer edges of the outriggers, allowing decent-sized footwells and acceptably accommodating rear seats. The main fore and aft chassis members were made from steel box sections and the outriggers were supported on three extensions on each side of the main members. The outriggers ran from the front of the footwell, behind the front wheel and along the outer edge of the body shell, then sloped inwards after the 'B' pillar to meet with the main chassis members just in front of the rear axle line. At the front of the unit, a fabricated steel box-section frame formed a pair of suspension towers, with the top of the towers joined together with a transverse bolt-on bracing strut to maintain rigidity, similar in layout to that seen on the Scimitar Coupé.

At the rear of the chassis, the main longitudinal members flared outwards and terminated just in front of the axle. A fabricated triangular box sat at the end of each longitudinal member, and smaller longitudinal members were welded to the top of the box structure to extend rearwards. A cross brace between the tops

LEFT: **The GTE's chassis was all new, and was longer and wider than the Scimitar's, but the Scimitar GT's suspension was retained. The 'X'-shaped central chassis rails and the outriggers are clearly visible.**

BELOW: **Bob Cole's very early GTE, pictured at the RSSOC 2017 Culborough Sprint. The contrast with the earlier Sabre Six is clear.**

of the boxes maintained rigidity, and the ends of the longitudinal rails were joined with a second cross-member, to form a square box that supported the body's boot floor. A short steel box section extended from the lower level of the fabricated box, and ran under the axle, and a vertical box section ran from the end of this element and joined the upper longitudinal rail, forming a square through which the axle ran. A bracing channel ran diagonally from the bottom of the structure up to the end of the main longitudinal rail, bracing the rear of the chassis structure.

At 17 gallons (77 litres), the fuel tank was smaller than the Scimitar GT's and was placed in the box formed by the two chassis longitudinal members, the differential cross-member and the rear cross-member. In this location, the chassis steelwork afforded the tank some protection in a crash. The chassis was lengthened and widened in comparison with the Scimitar unit, with the 99-inch (251.46-cm) wheelbase gaining 6.5 inches (16.5cm); the front track, at 55.6 inches (141.22cm), was widened by 4.1 inches (10.41cm); the rear track of 53.3 inches (135.38cm) was widened by 2.8 inches (7.11cm) in the rear to improve the car's lateral stability and maintain the wheelbase/track ratio.

The final difference from the Scimitar was the positioning of the spare wheel. In the GTE it was placed in the nose of the car, above the radiator, where it improved the fore and aft weight distribution and probably added some impact protection.

Body and Interior

The GTE's body shell was in the Reliant tradition – made from glass fibre and moulded in two halves. The outer half formed the outside of the car and a secondary inner half formed the floor, wheel-arch liners and internal bracing and footwells. A third, smaller moulding formed the dashboard and centre console. The three mouldings were bonded together to form a strong and rigid body shell, which was bolted to the chassis at nine points. Two bolts fixed the body to the front suspension legs, four bolts were positioned behind the rear seat wells, and another four were positioned in front of the rear trim panel. The seat mounts and the seat-belt reel mounts were bolted through the body shell into the chassis, and there was a single bolt on each side on the inside of the door steps. A pair of bolts were positioned on the centre console and a further pair were fitted in each front footwell. Finally, there were four bolts, two on each side, to secure the base of the roll-over hoop on to the chassis at the bottom of the 'B' pillar.

The body shell had two steel tube strengthening elements bonded in. A pair of 1-inch diameter steel tubes were welded together and formed into a loop, which followed the line of the 'B' post from the sill level, up the door 'B' pillar and over the roof to surround the passenger cell, forming a roll-over bar. These were bonded into the body and added torsional rigidity to the shell, and the base of each end was bolted to the chassis. Some sunroof installations removed the centre section of the hoop, and retaining the strength of the shell then relied on a properly installed sunroof surround. A second bonded-in 1-inch diameter tubular steel hoop ran up the door hinge posts, through the screen pillars and along the top of the windscreen, to provide further reinforcement of the shell.

The styling of the body shell was completely different from anything that had gone before, with two unique features that would define the GTE throughout its long life. The first was the upsweep of the rear wings, which successfully avoided the typical van-like appearance of conventional estate cars, and the second was the all-glass hatch, which gave unimpeded access to the long and flat load area.

Much thought and design inspiration had been applied to the interior of the GTE, to make it one of the outstanding features of the car. The new chassis, with its cruciform design, allowed the front and rear seats to be placed lower than in the Scimitar, and the extra length between the wheels meant there was more than adequate room for the four passengers'

The GTE has very clean lines, clearly derived from the Coupé but with a distinct and unique look. Neat but minimal chrome trim around the windows and a single waistline trim strip emphasize the car's simple but sophisticated style.

ABOVE: **The SE5a retained all of the early GTE's good looks. Shaun Pierce's car also shows how a bright colour can complement the car's lines.**

RIGHT: **The first GTE's interior was very similar to that of the later Scimitar Coupé. While the all-black finish is sombre, the overall feel is of a nice office in which to do some high-performance motoring.**

feet. The front seats were conventional and were trimmed in black Ambla plastic. They offered a good range of adjustment fore and aft, along with a lever-operated tilting backrest, which could go from vertical to almost horizontal. Both front seats tilted forwards on their front mounts to give access to the rear seats; alternatively, the seat's rear squab could be folded forwards to gain access. The faces of the rear seats were covered in Ambla plastic, to match the fronts, and the back of the seats was carpeted, to match the load bay.

One of the few complaints about the car's interior related to the pedals, with had been placed closer together than some journalists wanted, due to the transmission cover intruding into the footwell. The steering wheel had a leather-covered rim supported by two horizontal spokes, each drilled with four holes for lightness, and a padded 'safety' centre. A single stalk on the right-hand side operated the horn, dip and main beam, headlamp flash and indicators.

A fully equipped instrument panel, housed in a separate moulding, faced the driver. It was based on that of the Scimitar Coupé, retaining that car's 'flat plank of wood' layout, which was redolent of many 1960s British sports cars. The 4-inch diameter speedometer and rev counter were positioned directly in front of the driver, and straddled the 2-inch diameter gauges for coolant temperature and oil pressure. In the centre of the dashboard, another pair of 2-inch diameter instruments, an ammeter and fuel gauge, flanked a centrally mounted clock. All the instruments were supplied by Smiths Industries and all had white lettering on black dials and matt black rims. To the left of the minor instruments on the main dash were a pair of toggle switches for the rear wiper (when fitted) and instrument panel lights.

Below the three central instruments was a radio and to the left a glove box with lid. Below the radio was a vertical flat centre console, which carried all the minor switches and heater controls, as well as a cigar lighter. The heater itself was a relatively crude water-valve-controlled unit with little proper temperature control between hot and cold. The switches were

the traditional toggle type – soon to be outlawed on safety grounds in favour of flush-fitting rocker switches – and operated the lights, wipers and washers, instrument lights, heater fan, and a cigar lighter. Beneath these, there sat a pair of rotary heater controls. On each extremity of the facia was an eyeball-type air vent, which provided fresh air to the interior. The water-valve-controlled heater lived behind the dashboard and was considered to be pretty good by the standards of the time, providing reasonable defrosting for the windscreen and plenty of heat to the interior. Through-flow ventilation of the car was achieved by automatically extracting air from the interior. Discrete ventilator grilles on the rear sides of the body were sited in a low-pressure area when the car was moving, and were used to draw stale air out of the car via slots around the rear windows. There was an option to have the rear window electrically heated. Lap and diagonal seat belts were fitted to the front seats, and fixing points for rear belts were provided.

The two individual rear seats were heavily sculptured and sat on each side of the transmission tunnel, which carried an armrest. The seats were fixed in position but each individual backrest could be folded forwards to increase the size of the load bay. The backs were upholstered with carpet to match

The GTE's rear seats were significantly larger than the Scimitar Coupé's, with the width and legroom to make them comfortable for adults.

RIGHT: **With both folding rear seats down, the GTE offered an impressive luggage space of 36 cubic feet.**

BELOW: **The first brochure for the GTE made great play about its load-carrying capacity. The complex steel hatch supports were quickly replaced by gas struts on the production cars.**

the floor of the load bay, and had a strap-type handle on the back to assist in the pulling action – upward and forward – needed to hinge them forwards. The central armrest also hinged forwards on a substantial steel arm to provide a central 'stop', to prevent luggage sliding into the backs of the front seats when braking. The load area was fully carpeted, and the whole interior was comprehensively upholstered in black initially, including the headlining, with no exposed glass fibre to be found. The load area offered the

owner three combinations of passenger and luggage space. With both rear seats in use, the load bay offered 19cu ft/0.538cu m of load space; with one seat folded down, there was 27cu ft/0.765cu m; and with both seats folded down there was 36cu ft/1.019cu m in total.

While the front windows were manually operated at first, an electrically operated option was quickly offered. The front quarter-lights could also be opened manually to provide draught-free ventilation, but the rear windows were fixed in place. The top-hinged tailgate was made from a single large sheet of toughened glass, with a thin metal frame. Initially, it was supported on a complex mechanically assisted lifting mechanism, but, in another first from Reliant, this was rapidly replaced by a pair of gas struts, which assisted the opening of the hatch and also supported it when it was up.

Lighting was catered for at the front with four 5.5-inch (14-cm) diameter headlights each side of a dummy grille with four horizontal slats. The chrome front bumper was in two parts, curving around each corner, and each half was terminated with a Ford Escort over-rider just under the inboard headlamp, leaving a space for the number plate between the over-riders. The air intake was sited under the number plate. A dedicated indicator light nestled below each bumper, and there was a shield-shaped scimitar

ABOVE: **Bob Cole's GTE is early and original. Note the metal styling line along the car's waist – a distinctive feature of the early cars.**

LEFT: **The GTE's rear hatch was an integral part of both its styling and versatility.**

**The engine bay of Bob Cole's GTE, showing positioning
of the spare wheel and the V6, which is set well back.**

badge in the centre of the top panel just ahead of
the bonnet, and the word 'SCIMITAR' picked out in
individual chromed letters on the front panel above
the dummy grille. A rectangular '3-litre' badge was
placed on the front wing, behind the front wheel and
just below the moulded-in body line. Some cars came
with a three-piece chrome trim strip running on each
side just above the moulded-in cheat line.

The tailgate lock and catch were centrally located
above the fuel filler cap on the rear of the car. While
the tailgate opening was wide and gave good visibility
when reversing, the high loading sill came in for some
criticism from the press at the time. The one-piece
rear light clusters sat above the one-piece chrome
bumper and carried the rear and brake light, indicators
and reflector, and the number plate was fixed centrally
under the bumper with a reversing light on each end.
'SCIMITAR' was spelt out in individual letters above

the left-hand-side lamp cluster and there was a small
one-piece rectangular 'GTE' badge to its right; the later
cars had 'GTE' spelt in individual letters over the right-
hand-side tail light, and when appropriate a rectangular
'automatic' badge next to it.

Engine, Gearbox and Final Drive

Reliant capitalized on its experience gained with the
Scimitar by using the 3-litre Ford Essex V6 from the
Ford Zodiac Mk 4 in the GTE. Originally, Reliant intended to offer the Zephyr 2.5-litre V6 in the GTE too,
but demand for the 3-litre unit meant that this option
was quietly dropped when the car entered production.
In the GTE, the Ford V6 produced a healthy 144bhp
at 4,750rpm, along with an impressive 192.5lb/ft of
torque at 3,000rpm, which perfectly suited the GTE's
market position as a GT car. Excellent performance
was complemented by easy driving characteristics;

with the ample torque, pulling power was instantly available through virtually the whole rev range.

The car came with the standard Ford four-speed and reverse gearbox originally fitted to the V6-engined Zephyr, Zodiac and Transit, as used on the SE4b and c, with synchromesh on all four forward gears. A Ford 2604E overdrive unit could be ordered with the manual box.

Suspension

At the front, the GTE adopted the Scimitar's independent system from Alford and Alder, with its unequal-length twin wishbones, Triumph TR6-derived uprights with brass bottom trunnion fixed to the wishbones with nylon 'top hat' bushes, and a ball-joint top swivel. The live axle was essentially the Scimitar unit, but was slightly wider to give a more generous track. The wider track was achieved by introducing a wider chassis rather than by changing the length of the wishbones. At the rear, the live axle also adopted the same layout seen on the later Scimitars, with a pair of trailing arms on each side to control the axle's up-and-down movement, a pair of coil over dampers and a Watts linkage with a pair of radius arms locating the axle transversely. The GTE's trailing arms were lengthened by 8 inches (just over 20cm) in comparison with the Scimitar's units, which allowed more rear-wheel

Early cars came with steel wheels as standard and were fitted with these, now rare, glass-fibre wheel trims.

movement, and helped to give the GTE a softer but still well-controlled rear-suspension movement.

The rack-and-pinion steering had the rack mounted ahead of the axle line and was set up with no 'Ackermann' geometry. The GTE's geometry was set up to increase the slip angles of the steering wheels, which had the effect of increasing the cornering power of the front outside wheel and helped to give the GTE its good and predictable high-speed handling.

Brakes and Wheels

The GTE adopted the same braking system seen on the Scimitar Coupé, with hydraulically operated discs at the front and drums at the rear, and a cable-operated handbrake operating on the rear drums. The 10.63-inch (27cm) diameter front discs were gripped by Girling three-piston calipers. The rear drums were 9 inches in diameter with a width of 1.75 inches; both shoes were operated by a single hydraulic cylinder giving a single leading shoe.

The wheels as standard were 14-inch 5½J wide steel bolt-ons, initially fitted with glass-fibre wheel trims with a four-spoke pattern, with 185x14 Pirelli Cinturato radial tyres specified. Optional alloys with a complex eight-spoke design were soon specified, retaining the 185x14 tyres and four-bolt fixings.

Scimitar GTE Developments

After a year of production, an automatic version of the SE5 GTE was introduced at the October 1969 Earls Court Motor Show. The car used the well-proven Borg Warner 35 unit, a three-speed unit with torque converter. Additional refinements for the range included a rear wiper with electric washer, and the option of a higher-geared rear differential with a 3.31:1 drive ratio. The rear wiper was also available from Reliant as a retro-fit kit for earlier cars, and had two speeds. The interior changes included a revised safety steering wheel, designed to collapse forwards in the event of a collision and with energy-absorbing pads on the spokes. The safety-oriented makeover on the rest of the interior resulted in all surfaces being 'safety padded in black anti-dazzle trim'. The facia storage was improved and grab handles were fitted on the 'B' pillars to help the rear passengers in and out. The front seats were fully reclining Aero types, and the rear squabs were altered to match.

SCIMITAR GTE SE5A

In October 1971 Reliant carried out a series of re-vamps to the car, resulting in the SE5a. An all-new vacuum-formed ABS moulding gave the whole dash-board area an integrated appearance, taking the car away from the very 1960s 'flat plank of wood' ap-pearance of the SE5's dash. The new dash moulding had a flat recessed face in front of the driver, which ex-tended over the centre console, and a glove compart-ment in front of the passenger. The instruments were recessed into the flat panel and the top of the dash formed a hood, which helped to cut down reflections.

The 4-inch (10-cm) diameter speedometer and rev counter remained in front of the driver, flanking the 2-inch (5-cm) diameter temperature and oil-pressure gauges. The GTE driver was given plenty of warning lights: the speedo had the left-hand indicator and ignition charge lights at 5 and 7 o'clock, while the rev counter housed the right-hand indicator warning and high beam, again at 5 and 7 o'clock. Between the speedo and rev counter, under the temp and oil-pressure gauges, and in line with the driver's eye line, was a horizontal row of four additional rectan-gular warning lights. These indicated electric engine fan on, brake-pad wear, brake fluid low and low fuel. Three more 2-inch (5-cm) diameter minor instru-ments (voltmeter, clock and fuel gauge) were lined up on the dash above a radio slot, in line with the centre console. Below the instruments there was an

Later (in this case an SE5a) cars had a more sculpted dashboard, with the instruments recessed to cut down reflections and a sloping shelf to carry the rocker switches that were demanded by safety legislation.

ABOVE: **There are still many GTEs in use, much cherished by their owners. This nice SE5a was seen at the RSSOC Culborough Sprint.**

LEFT: **On the SE5a, the reversing lights were integrated into the rear light cluster and the badging was revised. Note also the air-extraction vents on the side of the car.**

almost horizontal flat platform, between the steering wheel and the glove box, and this carried four rocker switches for the lights, front and rear wipers, and the screen washers. The platform reappeared on the other side of the steering wheel, and carried another pair of rocker switches, which operated the heated rear screen and hazard warning lights.

The heating system had been reworked, with an air-blending unit replacing the simpler 'hot or cold' valve system of the SE5. The fresh-air-only dash-end eyeball vents of the SE5 had been repositioned on to the upper half of the centre console panel below the dash, flanking the two-speed heater fan rocker switch. Below them were the heater slide controls, with a rotary switch on the left-hand side to control the instrument illumination brightness, and a cigar lighter on the right-hand side.

The outside had been lightly revised for the SE5a. The headlamps were 2 inches (5cm) higher, to meet new regulations, and flanked a new dummy grille, now a one-piece casting with seven horizontal bars. At the rear, new light clusters incorporated the reversing light as the inboard lens. The badging was subtly different from the SE5: the '3-Litre' badges on the flanks were replaced by a shield-shaped Scimitar badge as seen on the front top panel, the 'SCIMITAR' lettering stayed on the nose above the grille, and at the rear, while the 'SCIMITAR' lettering remained on the left-hand-side back panel, the SE5's rectangular GTE badge had disappeared, to be replaced by the text 'GTE' on the right-hand side. Rectangular 'OVERDRIVE' or 'AUTOMATIC' badges were fitted to the right of the GTE characters depending on the specification level. As with the SE5, the Reliant name did not

**Although they are rare today, vinyl roofs were all the rage back in the 1970s.
The Scimitar's rising waistline made it hard to know where to fit one!**

SHAUN PIERCE – SCIMITAR GTE SE5A

Shaun Pierce's 1972 GTE is an SE5a model in April Yellow No. 2 (the same colour as the GTE on the cover of Don Pither's book), with brown leather interior, electric windows, 'Sundym' tinted glass and a four-speed manual gearbox with overdrive on third and top gears. He has owned the car since 1990, when it was traded in at his father's garage for another classic, and has carried out a full body-off restoration over a number of years.

The restoration covered everything: body off the chassis, chassis refurbished, all mechanical elements, brakes, suspension, engine refurbished, a full interior re-trim with new carpet, headlining and Jaguar XJS leather seats. The biggest job of the restoration was the stripping back of the body shell to the gel coat, which took some 120 hours to complete. The paintwork is holding up well and the car still looks stunning. Shaun puts this down to good preparation, ensuring the body shell was completely dry, and sealing all the interior surfaces and underside by painting them as well as the car's outside faces. The reasoning behind sealing the body shell is to prevent water getting into the structure after painting, which can cause blistering and lifting of the paint. The good condition of the paintwork is also due to there being only one colour coat on the car, which was sprayed on over a high build etch primer. As a result, there are no extra layers of paint or isolated repairs on the body, which can result in sinkage and cracking as the paint settles and the body 'moves' – as glass fibre is prone to doing.

Shaun replaced the original automatic gearbox with a manual and overdrive setup as he prefers the driving experience and the benefits of the overdrive, and when he did this he discovered that the automatic Scimitar's transmission tunnel was different to that of the manual and he had to cut out the original automatic one and glass in one from a scrapped manual car.

**Shaun Pierce uses his GTE for long-distance touring, often pulling
a classic 1970s folding caravan. The lusty V6 copes with ease.**

**Shaun Pierce's GTE was always intended to be a tourer – here it is by
the Lac du Salagou in the south of France, on the 2013 family holiday.**

The rebuilt engine was ported and gas flowed, the only job Shaun farmed out, it has the standard Weber carb and
a pair of tubular manifolds, and is still running beautifully. The cooling system came in for some attention, with the
radiator getting a re-core with an extra row, and a Kenlowe fan to increase airflow through the radiator. In addition,
Shaun regularly carries out a thorough flush out of the cooling system to keep it at peak efficiency. A new stainless
exhaust finished the engine side off, and Shaun has fitted new headlights and fully restored the rear lamp clusters,
so he can see and be seen at night. The bumpers were painted satin black for aesthetic reasons and the wheels are
US Indy Mags, which are Wolfrace lookalikes – in fact it appears that Wolfrace actually licensed the design from
American Racing Equipment in the 1970s. The wheels are fitted with stainless nuts to avoid the cracked chrome
and subsequent rust that the standard nuts suffer from.

Shaun uses his GTE as a reliable Grand Tourer – he really enjoys driving the car on long and short distances and
finds the handling is good and confidence inspiring; it is currently sitting on a set of Dunlop 'Sport Blu Response' tyres.
In Shaun's hands, the car lives up to its GTE label, as he has taken the car all over Europe, including Austria, Ireland,
Belgium, Germany and the south of France and it has never let him down – important when he has his family along
with him for the holidays! The only down side to the car is the lack of a decent sunroof or air conditioning means
the car gets hot when in the sunnier climes, but with the windows down and the car moving it's manageable – he just
has to avoid traffic jams! The car is a credit to Shaun's mechanical and restoration skills and the Reliant brand, and
demonstrates how the Scimitar can be a practical and attractive classic car in the right hands.

appear on the outside of the car. New Dunlop composite wheels, with alloy centres and steel rims, were offered to replace the all-alloy wheel option.

In 1972, Reliant adopted an uprated version of the Essex V6, which had a new, stronger block casting and improved porting. The new engine's sump necessitated changes to the chassis, with one of the crossmembers being replaced by a bolt-on plate; the engine mounts were also modified. The engine-mounted fan was replaced by an electric unit placed in front of the radiator and the removable top suspension turret

brace was also modified, to clear the new installation. Ford also discontinued the 2604E overdrive at this time, so Reliant fitted the four-speed Granada gearbox, and raised the axle ratio on the manual cars to the 3.07 ratio used in the automatics, to keep the high top gear. Unfortunately, this meant that the first gear had become quite high, which could cause problems when towing, especially during hill starts. The problem was fixed by the use of a Laycock J-type overdrive with a Ford Special Vehicles Operations (SVO) sourced gearbox, usually seen in police and ambulance Transit vans.

SCIMITAR SE5 SPECIFICATIONS

	Scimitar SE5 – Manual/overdrive	**Scimitar SE5a – Automatic**
Layout and chassis	Three-door four-seat coupé/estate. Glass-fibre body shell, steel chassis	Three-door four-seat coupé/estate. Glass-fibre body shell, steel chassis
Engine	Ford Essex 3.0	Ford Essex 3.0
Type	V6	V6
Block material	Cast iron	Cast iron
Head material	Cast iron	Cast iron
Cylinders	6	6
Cooling	Pressurized water and antifreeze mix	Pressurized water and antifreeze mix
Bore and stroke	93.67 x 72.42mm	93.67 x 72.42mm
Capacity	2994cc	2994cc
Valves	Two per cylinder	Two per cylinder
Compression ratio	8.9:1	8.9:1
Carburettor	Twin-choke Weber 40DFA-1	Twin-choke Weber 40DFA-1
Max power (claimed)	138bhp @ 4,500rpm	144bhp @ 4,750rpm
Max torque	172lb/ft @ 3,000rpm	192.5lb/ft @ 3,000rpm
Fuel capacity	17 gallons/77.3 litres	17 gallons/77.3 litres
Transmission		
Gearbox	Ford four-speed with optional overdrive on 3rd and 4th (0.82:1)	Borg Warner 35 three-speed automatic
Clutch	Single plate, diaphragm spring	Single plate, diaphragm spring
Ratios		
1st	3.346:1	2.47:1
2nd	2.214:1	1.47:1
3rd	1.412 (o/d 1.16:1):1	1.0:1
4th	1.0 (o/d 0.82:1):1	n/a
Reverse	3.346:1	2.11:1
Final drive	3.58:1	3.07:1

SUMMARY

As a completely new class of car, the GTE was a re-sounding success for Reliant. The whole concept of the car was validated by good sales and the car was very well received by customers and the contemporary press. The concept was picked up by various manufacturers – Volvo with the P1800ES in 1972, the Lancia Beta HPE in 1975, and even the two-seat Jensen Healey GT of 1975 – but probably the main rival for the GTE was Ford's Capri, which from its Mark 2 incarnation of 1974 featured a hatchback. However, the GTEs combination of exclusivity, performance, space and versatility, allied to its ability to cover considerable distances in comfort and the long-lasting corrosion-free glass-fibre body shell meant that the car continued to be seen as something just a bit special.

The SE5 was produced between 1968 and 1975, and was produced in two versions – the SE5 (1968–1971) of which 2,469 were build, and the SE5a (1971–1975) of which 6,635 were produced, giving a grand total of 9,104 cars.

	Scimitar SE5 – Manual/overdrive	Scimitar SE5a – Automatic
Suspension and steering		
Suspension front	Triumph-based independent double wishbone, coil springs and damper, anti-roll bar	Triumph-based independent double wishbone, coil springs and damper, anti-roll bar
Suspension rear	Live rear axle, twin trailing arms and Watts linkage. Coil over dampers	Live rear axle, twin trailing arms and Watts linkage. Coil over dampers
Steering	–	–
Tyres	185x14 radial	185x14 radial
Wheels	5.5J x 14in pressed steel	5.5J x 14in pressed steel
Brakes		
Type	Disc front, drum rear	Disc front, drum rear
Size: front	10.63in/27cm diameter	10.63in/27cm diameter
Size: rear	9in /22.8cm diameter 1.75in/4.45cm width	9in /22.8cm diameter 1.75in/4.45cm width
Dimensions		
Track: front	55in/139.7cm	55in/139.7cm
Track: rear	53in/134.6cm	53in/134.6cm
Wheelbase	99.5in/252.7cm	99.5in/252.7cm
Overall length	171in/434.3cm	171in/434.3cm
Overall width	64.5in/163.8cm	64.5in/163.8cm
Overall height	52in/132cm	52in/132cm
Kerb weight	2,542.4lb/1,153kg	2,766.4lb/1,254kg
Performance		
Top speed	120mph/193km/h	117mph/188km/h
0–60mph	10.2 secs	13.2 secs

CHAPTER 5

A BIGGER ESTATE AND A CONVERTIBLE:

THE SCIMITAR GTE SE6 (1975–1986), GTC SE8 (1980–1986) AND MIDDLEBRIDGE GTE (1988–1990)

THE SE6 SERIES

Moving Upmarket

After the SE5 had been in production for six years, Reliant carried out a major update of the GTE, which resulted in the introduction in 1975 of the SE6 model. Reliant announced the new GTE with the strap line 'A Bigger All-Round Motoring Experience'. Wider and longer than the SE5, the SE6 offered more room for its four passengers and a 10 per cent increase in

With the SE6 version of the GTE, Reliant made the car longer and wider but retained the classic lines.

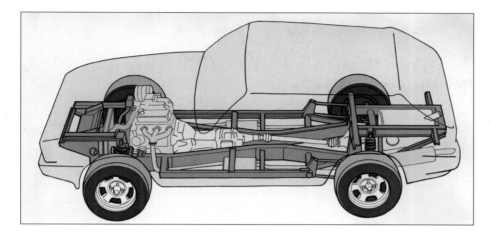

With its longer and wider chassis, the SE6 offered increased interior space and a larger overall profile.

luggage capacity, to move the car further upmarket and cement its place as the best estate car in the GT class. The SE6 retained the original GTE's layout and appearance but, by adding about 3.5 inches (9cm) to the overall length and 3 inches (7.5cm) to the overall width and introducing some subtle styling changes, Reliant made a car that was both more imposing and recognizably different from the original SE5. Tom Karen of Ogle Design was the main inspiration behind the changes, coming up with a neat update to the classic SE5 lines that would see Reliant safely into the 1980s.

SE6 Chassis

The SE6 chassis layout was the same as the SE5 unit, retaining the cruciform main chassis legs and still constructed from steel 'U' and box sections. To provide the additional width and length needed, the fore and aft chassis members that made up the central cruciform were spaced apart by an extra 3 inches (7.5cm) when compared with the SE5, and had an additional 4 inches (10cm) of length added between the wheels. The outriggers were also lengthened and were connected to the central cruciform by a cross-member front and rear and two cross-members in the midsection – one positioned alongside the gearbox and one at the tail of the gearbox (the SE5 only had one).

One advantage of the extra width of the chassis was that there was now space to put a larger fuel tank between the rear legs, giving an extra 3 gallons (13.6 litres) and raising the overall capacity to an impressive 20 gallons (91 litres). The front and rear

suspension layouts remained the same as on the SE5, although the spring and damper rates were altered to give the SE6 a softer and more comfortable ride. This was in line with the car's elevation further up the GT market – Reliant wanted to provide a soft and well-controlled ride to its new customer, who was perceived to be more sophisticated and perhaps less sporting.

SE6 Body and Interior

Despite the update, the new car managed to retain the original car's distinctive flowing lines and overall appearance, while looking much more contemporary. In terms of styling, the exterior of the SE6 featured a number of differences when compared with the SE5. At the front, new squared-off black GRP bumpers, with rubber inserts and bright metal top trims, replaced the SE5's chromed quarter units, and the 5.75-inch (14.5-cm) diameter outer headlamps were replaced by larger, 7-inch (18-cm) diameter units. A bright metal plate with 'SCIMITAR' embossed in it sat on the top of the central fake grille, which had five slats and a black finish.

The raised centre strip on the SE5's bonnet and front panel became much wider, spanning the width of the car between the headlights, and a sunken centre strip ran the whole length of the bonnet, terminating halfway along the front of the top panel with a Scimitar badge. The whole front end was bluffer than the SE5's, and gave the car a more imposing appearance. At the rear, GRP bumpers with rubber inserts again replaced the chromed steel blade of the SE5,

**Two-tone paintwork became popular in the 1970s and 1980s. This GTE features
the typical contrasting stripe paintwork that Reliant offered as an option.**

and the corner air-extractor vents were covered with black plastic trim. A new, almost flush-fitting fuel filler cap was fitted in the middle of the rear panel, and the rear bumper had a central recess for the rear number plate, capped with a raised length and a chromed trim along its top. The big new bumpers were a major styling factor, and their presence was instrumental in giving the car a much more modern appearance than the SE5. To meet new safety requirements, flush-fitting door handles were sourced from the British Leyland parts bin (and shared with the Lotus Elite, which was new at the time), replacing the SE5's chromed push-button items. Finally, a subtle lower styling line was moulded into the body and doors at roughly the same level as the top of the bumpers, which helped to stiffen the body shell and emphasize the new lines of the car.

Despite the overall exterior dimensions changing only slightly, the most important revisions were made by increasing the track by 3 inches (7.5cm) and

**John Unwin's SE6b shows
the revised headlamps and
more aggressive and modern
stance of the SE6.**

The load bay of the SE6 was larger than that of the SE5. The factory also provided a folding cover for the bay, to conceal the contents.

the wheelbase by 4 inches (10cm). These increases were directly reflected in the interior, especially in the rear, giving the occupants significantly more room than the SE5a. The rear passengers had 4 inches (10cm) more legroom and front and rear occupants gained 3 inches (7.5cm) of elbow room. The extra length of the cabin also meant the door length was increased, which allowed easier entry into and exit from the cabin, especially the rear. The larger cabin extended into the load area as well, giving a significant increase in luggage capacity. With both the rear seats in use, the SE6 offered 21cu ft/0.595cu m of luggage space (which had been 19cu ft/0.538cu m in the SE5); with one seat down, this increased to 30cu ft/0.85cu m (SE5: 27cu ft/0.765cu m); with both seats down, the car offered 40cu ft/1.133cu m (SE5: 36cu ft/ 1.019cu m).

As well as the improved seating space, there were extensive updates to the other interior features, to help move the car upmarket. An all-new dashboard moulding had fresh-air eyeball vents at each end and a recessed panel in front of the driver, carrying the 4-inch (10-cm) diameter Smiths speedometer and tachometer, with a Triumph-sourced 'all systems go' warning light cluster – a circular display incorporating eight warning lights for ignition on/charging, low fuel, left- and right-hand indicators, hand brake on, choke on, oil pressure and high beam between the instruments. The top half of the centre console housed a row of four 2-inch (5-cm) diameter Smiths gauges for battery condition in volts, water temperature,

fuel level and oil pressure. Below sat the clock and a radio. All the instruments and the clock had white lettering on a black background, white needles and satin black bevels. Below the radio was a flat panel, angled at about 45 degrees, which carried two blocks of two rocker switches, which operated the heated rear window, hazards, lights and rear fog lights. The steering column had two stalks, the left-hand side controlling the windscreen wipers and washers, the right-hand side for headlamp dip, main and flash and indicators. Below the switches was a centre console, with a pair of fresh-air eyeball vents, the heater slide controls and the panel lights' rheostat and the rear wiper/washer switch mounted on it. At the base of the centre console there was a cigar lighter and ash tray, and finally, in front of the passenger, there was a lockable glove box.

The heating and ventilation system was thoroughly updated. The new heater followed the practice of the time, which had a heater matrix permanently plumbed into the cooling system and blending the amount of air passed through it to control the temperature. It was in stark contrast to the on or off water-valve system used on the SE5. The external air supply was revised, with a pair of inlet pipes positioned behind each set of headlamps, and a dedicated electric fan for each inlet. This meant there was a more than adequate supply of air into the system. In the cabin, fresh-air ventilation was supplied via four eyeball vents, two in the centre console and one at each end of the dash. Fresh air was ducted

The interior of the SE6 built on the design of the SE5, updating it to give a more modern appearance.

over the heater matrix and was directed to ducts to the windscreen and/or the front footwells, as required. The ventilation system was deemed to be good enough, so the front-door quarter-lights were fixed, as were the rear side windows. Stale air was extracted through larger modified vents on the rear sides of the car, fed from interior ducts in the rear of the cabin.

The seats were upholstered with cloth faces and buttoned velour pleating, while the sides were covered in vinyl, with most cars being delivered with tan-coloured interiors.

SE6 Mechanicals

Mechanically, the car continued with a very similar specification to the SE5a, with the Ford Essex 3-litre V6, and the same gearbox options of manual, manual and overdrive or automatic. The Borg Warner automatic box of the SE5 was replaced by the Ford C3 unit, which was still a three-speed (plus reverse) unit but was generally a much more up-to-date design than the 1960s Borg Warner unit. The main change to the engine was a revised cooling system, which became a fully sealed system with an expansion tank. This system was never really satisfactory, especially as the positioning of the header tank meant that there could be problems with water circulation to the inlet manifold. This gave the SE6 (and the SE6a) a reputation for overheating once the cars had been in use for a few years.

The rear axle was wider, to allow for the increased track and cabin width, and ZF power steering was listed as an option. The front suspension retained the TR6-derived twin-wishbone set-up of the SE5, but with softer springs and damping. A power-assisted steering system, made by ZF, was offered and the rear also retained the twin trailing arms and Watts linkage of the SE5.

UPGRADING THE GTE: THE SE6A AND SE6B MODELS

Unfortunately, after the SE6 was placed in production, a number of issues arose with the handling and general refinement of the car. These were due to a combination of inadequate development and the increased expectations of the customers at whom the car was now aimed. While SE5 customers were buying a sporting GT car with some rough edges, the SE6 was marketed as a sophisticated and refined Grand Tourer – those rough edges would not be tolerated by the new clientele. The revised front suspension settings were too soft for many customers, resulting in complaints about the handling being imprecise and prone to bottoming out. The power steering was criticized for being too light and not offering much (if any) feel. The longer and wider chassis and body were not as rigid as the SE5's, and tended to flex, resulting in creaks and groans. Finally, the longer and heavier doors were much more prone to drooping.

RIGHT: **As with the SE5, the SE6's V6 was buried under the bulkhead, with the spare wheel mounted ahead of it. This is John Unwin's Cologne V6-powered SE6b.**

BELOW: **The SE6 may be bigger and heavier than the SE5, but owners are still happy to put the car through its paces on the track. This SE6 was pictured at the RSSOC 2017 Culborough Sprint.**

The First Iteration – The SE6a

The first revision of the SE6 was, in Reliant's standard coding, the SE6a, introduced to the market during 1976. The changes were mainly engineering upgrades to the body shell and suspension, to resolve the issues that had emerged in the production SE6. To address the flexing body shell and drooping doors, the steel reinforcement bonded into the scuttle and 'A' pillars was beefed up, which appeared to cure the problem. The power-assisted steering pump was modified to reduce the power delivered to the rack; this made the system heavier, but also gave more feel. It also had the unintended benefit of improving the rack seal's life.

As well as upgrading the steering and body, Reliant also turned its attention to the brakes. The front brakes were revised, with smaller, 10.5-inch diameter discs and two-piston calipers replacing the larger, 10.82-inch diameter discs and three-pot calipers of the SE6. At the rear, Lockheed 10-inch diameter by 1.75-inch width drums from the MGB replaced the 9-inch Girling units previously fitted.

The only visible upgrade on the SE6a was the inclusion of Wolfrace five-slot alloy wheels on the optional extras list, as Dunlop was ceasing production of its steel/alloy composite wheels.

Following these modifications, the SE6a was a success, and would remain in production until 1979.

The SE6's nose styling was distinctive, with its two different-sized headlamps.

The Second Iteration – The SE6b

In 1980, Reliant saw the writing on the wall for the long-in-the-tooth Essex 3-litre V6, and decided to replace it with the German-built Cologne 2.8-litre V6. This 60-degree all-iron V6 actually displaced 2792cc with a bore and stroke of 93 x 68.5mm. It had a five main bearing crankshaft, a cast-iron block and cylinder heads and was lighter than the Essex unit. The lighter engine meant the SE6b's weight was reduced by some 50lb (22.6kg), so the front spring and damper rates had to be changed to compensate. The cooling system was revised to be a fully pressurized system, with a properly positioned header tank, solving the cooling issues of the Essex-engined versions. The version fitted in the SE6b was equipped with a Solex carburettor with an automatic choke, and the unit produced 135bhp at 5,500rpm. One important aspect of the Cologne unit was that it produced less torque than the 3-litre Essex V6; to compensate for this, Reliant lowered the gearing, which made the engine seem slower than it actually was, lacking the easy, long-legged feel of the earlier engine. The distributor on the Cologne engine was fitted to the rear of the block, which meant in the GTE's installation it was buried under the bulkhead and pretty inaccessible. To lessen the impact of this unfortunate feature, all SE6bs were fitted with maintenance-free electronic ignition.

The SE6b's body shell also benefited from the company's experience of strengthening the GTC's shell, with the SE6b having a development of the GTC's steel scuttle reinforcing hoop fitted. The centre of this was bolted to the chassis, giving a useful increase in stiffness to the body shell. Externally, the SE6b had minor styling changes to differentiate the new model and tidy up the design. The front grille was changed for an all-black unit, which lost the bright strip with 'SCIMITAR' lettering. A new front chin spoiler sat under the front bumper and the lower styling line on the body sides got stick-on black rubber rubbing strips. The company also offered a two-tone paint scheme, with a broad band of colour down each flank to contrast with the main colour.

The final significant change to the SE6b was the introduction of a fully galvanized chassis. This occurred towards the end of production, but the exact date of introduction is not known.

THE SCIMITAR GTC SE8

A Crop-Topped GTE

Despite the country's inclement weather, the British public has a long-standing affection for convertibles. To address this unlikely preference, the post-war British car industry had a long pedigree of designing and producing four-seater convertible versions of bread-and-butter saloon cars during the 1950s and 1960s, with examples such as Ford's Zephyr, the Morris 1000 and Sunbeam's Rapiers. The affliction also spread to the monied classes, with a number of upmarket offerings from the likes of Alvis, Bentley and Rolls-Royce.

RELIANT EXPERIENCES

JOHN UNWIN'S 1982 SCIMITAR GTE SE6B

John Unwin, the Reliant Sabre and Scimitar Owners' Club Secretary, owns a lovely 1982 Scimitar GTE SE6b. With a Champagne exterior and tan interior, the car is smart and understated, and its Ford 2.8 Cologne V6 and manual gearbox with overdrive give it the performance to keep up with modern-day traffic as well as long legs for touring.

John's route to his current car has been very Reliant-oriented. As a broke and impecunious student who was sick of getting wet and cold on motorbikes, John bought his first Reliant, a 1957 Regal Mark 3 three-wheeler, because it could be driven on his motorbike licence and had a roof (well, a decent soft top) to keep the rain off! The lack of a heater meant he was still cold, but at least he kept dry. The car convinced him of the advantages of a solid chassis and rot-free glass-fibre bodywork and he continued to buy and drive later models of the Regal after he left university and entered the workplace. In 1973 he went on to four wheels, with a new Rebel.

One day, while in the showroom of local Reliant dealer Derek Warburton, in Stockport, John was introduced to the appealing new Scimitar GTE SE5a. His dream of owning one came true in 1978 after he had moved south to Woodley near Reading, and a new job paying more money put a second-hand SE5a within reach. Reliant dealer SGT in Taplow sold him a lovely 1972 SE5a – MMO 4L – a car he would dearly love to rediscover. The car had to go when his third child came along in 1981, so for a while he was without a GTE, but he always harboured a desire to have another. In 1997, coincidentally on his twenty-fifth wedding anniversary, his wife Jill showed him an advert for an SE6b and suggested that they go immediately to see it in Wiltshire. Leaving his four children to sort out the anniversary celebrations, John and Jill headed west; on seeing the car, they bought it there and then – quite an anniversary present.

**From the rear the extra width and longer
wheelbase do not detract from the SE6's lines.**

(continued overleaf)

JOHN UNWIN'S 1982 SCIMITAR GTE SE6B

The joy of buying the car was slightly tempered when its cooling system failed on the way home from picking it up, resulting in a big cloud of steam on the Black Dam roundabout in Basingstoke. The rest of the trip home was taken at a more sedate pace, with frequent stops to replenish the radiator. John knew that a fifteen-year-old used car would be sure to have some problems – and indeed there were a few. During his first two to three years of ownership, the GTE let him down several times, but its reliability increased as he went through the car, replacing worn or faulty parts and getting it into its current excellent state. A new radiator, water pump and housing, and coolant hoses sorted out the overheating. A complete overhaul of the front suspension, including setting up the geometry using a borrowed set of Dunlop gauges, made sure it was spot on, and the brakes were fully overhauled, with new pipes, cylinders, pads and shoes, with grooved and drilled front discs also fitted. Underneath, all was not well, so John replaced the corroded outriggers with new galvanized units.

As time went on, he continued to work through the car, refurbishing or replacing many more items, including brake and clutch master cylinders, heater blower motors, power steering rack, engine cooling fan and controller, door window frames and windscreen-wiper wheel boxes. All this work led to a car that was trustworthy and capable of reliable long-distance cruising, and handled nicely.

After all the work carried out on the car in his first few years of ownership, John experienced one major mechanical glitch. The engine was tired when he bought the car, so he replaced it after a year or so with a refurbished unit. At the same time, he refurbished the gearbox and propellor shaft and fitted a new clutch. Unfortunately, the new engine's fibre timing wheel broke up when he was on holiday ten years after fitting, resulting in an extended trip home with caravan courtesy of a yellow taxi! The necessary rebuild, to replace the fibre timing wheel with an alloy one, also enabled John to refresh the engine with new main and big-end shells as well as a new camshaft. Today it is running nicely, with good oil pressure and no apparent problems.

Cosmetically, the car has always looked good, but it was treated to a respray in 2013 to freshen it up. Further modifications have enhanced its reliability and convenience. These have included the fitting of a Revotec electric cooling fan controller, to replace the Kenlowe original; the more efficient Revotec unit is a nicely engineered device, which fits in line in the cooling hose, whereas the capillary tube of the Kenlowe had to slide in between the hose and radiator. The electrics have come in for some close attention, with a new modern blade-type fuse box, numerous relays to cut the current going through the ignition switch and dashboard switches and electronic remote central locking and alarm, using Maplin's door solenoids. New rear light units were sourced from eBay – the new units are brighter than the originals and, with the lenses attached by screws, allow bulbs to be changed from the outside, rather than having to dismantle the interior trim to access them, as on the standard units.

There have been a couple of downsides – the 40-foot (12-metre) turning circle is far too big and the fuel economy could be better, but these are minor matters compared to the pleasure John and Jill get from touring and driving the car. Seen regularly at RSSOC events, John's GTE is a credit to him, the club and Reliant. It is a car that continues to fulfil its design brief thirty-five years after it was built, and still gives its long-term owner a great deal of pleasure. Who could ask more of a car than that?

The fashion for affordable convertibles faltered in the 1960s, as the mainstream manufacturers renewed their ranges, and decided that developing convertible versions of the new models was not financially viable. Although it never actually happened, the prospect of the US market banning open cars, mooted in the late 1960s, was not encouraging either.

As a result, the only British mainstream-manufacturer four-seater convertible at the start of the 1970s was the Triumph Stag. Despite the Stag being discontinued in 1977, a victim of poor sales engendered by a reputation for fragile engines with cooling issues, Reliant still believed that there was a small but significant market in the UK for a four-seat convertible. The

With its hood up, the GTC can look a bit ungainly, but the car was an excellent four-seat convertible, and virtually unique in the market.

company also reasoned that the Scimitar GTE, with its robust chassis, could form a good basis for just such a car. The result was the Scimitar GTC, which appeared in 1980. Very much in the Stag idiom, and even using a hood mechanism developed from the Stag's, the GTC was more than just a crop-topped GTE.

Design and Development

The GTC was a proper four-seat convertible, with all the credentials that a proper grand tourer needed: a comfortable ride, good performance, plenty of space for four passengers and their luggage, a decent range and good looks. Building on the GTE's chassis and running gear, the rear end of the body shell was completely redesigned to provide seating for two rear-seat passengers, a well for the hood to fit into when down and a decent-sized boot. To help with this redesign, and to compensate for the loss of the roof, which in the GTE provided a significant element of strength to the shell, the GTC's body shell received substantial additional steel bracing. The GTE's roll bar was retained, and this was joined to the centre top of the windscreen with a pair of steel

The GTC looked better with the hood down. The sleek lines of Graham Fradgley's GTC are emphasized by the two-tone paint finish.

ABOVE LEFT: **The interior of the GTC was much the same as that of the GTE. The 'T' bar, which gave the occupants protection if the car rolled over and increased the body's rigidity, was pure Triumph Stag.**

ABOVE RIGHT: **The GTC's doors had strong location clips above the locks, which slotted into a fitting on the 'B' pillar to help with the strength of the passenger tub.**

tubes, forming the distinctive 'T' bar over the GTC's cockpit. A substantial 'U'-section steel upright was installed inside the 'A' pillars, the tops of which were connected across the car with a square-section steel tube running along the scuttle, and the door hinges were bolted to the upright. The scuttle bar was fixed to the chassis on each side of the transmission tunnel with a pair of vertical tubes, the bottoms of which were connected together with a horizontal tube. This feature was also fitted to the later SE6 GTE.

The windscreen uprights and top rail were also re-inforced, with square-section tubing in the uprights and round tubing in the top rail. The upright tubes were welded to the top rail tube, and were fixed to the 'A' pillar uprights, and carried forwards and down to meet the chassis just behind the wheels. The doors were positively located when closed by a neat lugged catch on the closing plate, which located in a casting bolted to the 'B' pillar. Finally, an 'N'-shaped reinforcing structure built from square-section steel tube was positioned just in front of the rear wheels, with its top bonded to the body just ahead of the boot-lid line, which bolted to the chassis to stiffen

up the rear end. The GTC retained the GTE's pair of fold-down rear seats, and a full-sized hatch gave access from the boot to the body when one or both of the seats were down. The dashboard, seats and other interior fittings were the same as those fitted to the GTE SE6b.

The GTC's hood was developed from the Stag item. Probably the most important element of a convert-ible is the hood – it has to look good when up and make the car look even better when down. To this end, most of the better convertibles conceal their hood and mechanism when closed. The Stag's unit dropped into a well beside and between the rear seats, where it was covered by a flush-fitting rigid cover, avoiding the raised 'pram hood' syndrome of some convertibles and presenting a smooth, flat rear deck. The GTC's hood followed this example, but, while it folded down into a well behind and beside the rear seats, rather than having a complicated hinged rigid cover it was covered by a tailored pop-on cover, which was made in the same material as the hood.

The front mechanism for securing the hood rail to the top of the windscreen varies on the GTC; early

ABOVE: **From the rear quarter, it is easy to see the changes that were needed to give the GTC a boot.**

LEFT: **Reliant did not exactly pull out all the stops when it came to styling the hard top, but it did at least make the interior of the GTC waterproof and warm in the winter months.**

ones had over-centre clips engaging on lugs on the rear face of the windscreen surround, as used on the MGB; while later ones had Triumph TR6/Stag/Spitfire peg-type levers, which engaged in a round hole on the top of the screen surround and used a cam action to clamp the hood rail to the top of the windscreen rail.

Reliant introduced an optional hard top for the GTC at the October 1980 London Motor Show held at Earls Court. It was a glass-fibre unit, with the exterior clad in textured black vinyl, and a fully trimmed interior. The rear window was heated, and the wiring, switch and warning light (which fitted in the centre console) was supplied with the top. The complete unit weighed 66lb (30kg) and was fitted using the two

clips on the windscreen rail and four bolts on the rear quarter panel. The top was designed to fit over the hood in its stowed position. The top followed the lines of the hood, and had two large side windows and chrome trim strips following the top of the door and the rear window. With its relatively large glass area, the hard top did not restrict visibility and made the GTC an attractive year-round car.

Modifications to the GTC while in production were few, but the cars did get a galvanized chassis at the same time as the GTE SE6b. Under the new body shell the GTC was identical to the GTE, with its independent front suspension, live rear axle and Ford Cologne 2.8 V6 mated to a four-speed manual or three-speed automatic gearbox.

RELIANT EXPERIENCES

GUY BETTS – GTC AND SCIMITAR COUPÉ SE4

Guy Betts owns two Reliants – a 1966 Scimitar Coupé SE4 and a 1981 GTC. The Coupé is a long-term restoration project; Guy bought it in 1988, and the restoration has been running since then as important life events – house moves, marriage and kids -- have taken precedence. Now, he is cracking on with the work and hopes to complete the car in the next year or so. The car is a late SE4, with the straight-six engine, and has chassis number 257 out of the 297 built before the V6-engined SE4a appeared. It exhibits some interesting original features that were standard on the SE4a. Their existence implies that the suspension modifications to the Coupé, done by John Crosthwaite, were introduced before production of the SE4a had started.

Guy's car has the SE4a-style rear suspension, with its two parallel trailing arms to locate the rear axle, and the front suspension wishbone mounts on the chassis are inside the box section, not on top as in the SE4 or mounted on the side as on the SE4a. The front suspension also sports an anti-roll bar, although the early-style vertical links are still fitted. The chassis does not show any signs of modification, so Guy strongly suspects that these alterations were done at the factory; examination of another unmolested late car's chassis a few years ago showed the same fittings. The final inconsistency is seen in the body and dash mouldings; while the car's original dashboard does not have the SE4a's eyeball vents at each end, the moulding does incorporate the ducting required to fit the vents.

Guy Betts stands by his GTC at Silchester Roman Town.

The restoration has reached a stage at which everything bar the body shell has been stripped, cleaned, repaired and restored. The body shell has been stripped and just needs a few minor repairs before it can be flatted down and prepared for paint. Its owner is very much looking forward to getting down to reassembling the car, once the shell has its new coat.

Unlike the Coupé, Guy's GTC, bought in October 2016, is a runner. While it is not his daily driver, he does use it to drive to meets and shows, and for days out with the roof down – when the British climate allows! Following ownership of a couple of SS1s in the 1980s and 90s, Guy decided that the time had come for another classic Reliant. The GTC came up at the right price and the right time. Mechanically, he has done some work on the front suspension, electrics, cooling system and fitted new tyres, as well as sorting out the lights and seat belts. Now he has taken the car to the high end of 'Condition 2'. It is not concours, but it is all up together and reliable, with everything working, and just a few minor cosmetic and mechanical issues that will be sorted over the next few months. Although he has owned it for only a few months, he has already built up some great memories with the car, including enjoying some excellent weather with the hood down, and, best of all, taking his son to his prom and being surrounded by some very exotic machinery and not feeling out of place. All in all, he is very pleased with the GTC, which makes a great companion car to his Coupé.

Guy Betts' GTC is usually driven with the roof down and makes a fine long-distance tourer.

THE MIDDLEBRIDGE GTE

After production of the GTE and GTC was discontinued, in November 1986, Nottingham-based businessmen John McCauley and Peter Boam approached Reliant with a view to buying the rights to the designs, along with the existing tooling. By mid-1987 they had negotiated a deal. With finance from Koji Nakauchi, who owned the Middlebridge group of companies, the rights and tooling to the GTE and GTC were purchased for £400,000 and a new company, Middlebridge Scimitar Ltd, was formed to produce the cars. New premises at Beeston, Nottingham were procured and, with significant investment from the Middlebridge Group, and moulds, tooling and jigs supplied by Reliant, prototyping was carried out. The new Scimitar GTE was launched in 1988, with an updated specification designed to move the car upmarket.

The new GTE had an estimated 450 changes when compared with the last of the Reliant-built cars, and was successfully put through UK type approval before proceeding to production.

The major changes included a fully galvanized chassis, the use of the then-current Ford Cologne 2.9 V6 with electronic fuel injection (the Reliant-built GTE and GTC had been fitted with the 2.8 version), a Ford five-speed manual or four-speed automatic gearbox, revised front and rear suspension, including a rear roll bar, and fire-resistant resin for the body shell. A myriad of minor changes was also made, either to improve the quality of the product, update the specification or to use currently available components. For example, VDO instruments replaced the original Smiths gauges, as they had better anti-glare properties. Smiths had also been reluctant to continue producing individual instruments as demand was decreasing. New, larger, rear light clusters were also fitted, along with halogen headlamps. These, along with the all-new impact-resistant bumpers, brought the car up to date. The car was fitted with its own design of 6J 15-inch diameter multi-spoked alloy wheels, fitted with 195VR 65x15 tyres. The Middlebridge wheels are now a popular fitment on earlier Scimitars, as they had the same offset and bolt pattern and there is a good range of modern tyres available in that size. Ford assisted with the installation of the engine, conducting cooling tests that resulted in the specification of a larger-capacity radiator than that sported by the SE6.

Customers began to take delivery of production cars during 1988. The various improvements to the car, along with the high-quality finish and fittings, made the Middlebridge Scimitar a desirable vehicle, but its appeal seemed to be somewhat limited in the late 1980s. Low order numbers, along with various issues

Middlebridge put the Scimitar GTE back into production in the late 1980s. With over 400 changes to the original, this was no mean feat.

The Middlebridge retained the GTE's good looks and, with its Ford 2.9-litre V6, added some performance as well.

with the parent company, led to the ceasing of production in 1990. Middlebridge did start to produce a single GTC, using a left-hand-drive GTC body shell sourced from Reliant, but that car was not completed.

With a production run of some seventy-nine cars, the Middlebridge Scimitar was a gallant effort to update the GTE and keep it in production. Production rights were then bought by Graham Walker Ltd, which still has the capability to build new GTEs and fully restore both Reliant and Middlebridge GTEs and GTCs.

NUMBERS: THE GTE AND GTC

The SE6 GTE and SE8 GTC enjoyed healthy sales in the 1970s and early 1980s, but sales were dropping off and the designs were ageing by the middle of the decade. Reliant took the decision to concentrate on the upcoming Small Sports project, and production of the GTE and GTC ended in November 1986.

The Middlebridge GTE took the car even further upmarket, but the financial woes of the parent company and relatively low sales meant that cars were produced only for a couple of years.

The SE6 was produced between 1975 and 1986, in three versions: the SE6 (1975–1976), of which 551 were build, the SE6a (1976–1979), of which 3,907 were produced, and the SE6b (1979–1986), of which 407 were produced, giving a grand total of 4,865 cars. The GTC was made between 1980 and 1986, with a total of 443 (including one prototype) made. The Middlebridge GTE was made between 1988 and 1990, with a total of eighty-three cars built, made up of seventy-nine production cars, two prototypes, one development car and one incomplete GTC.

John Unwin's SE6b illustrates the SE6 series well.

GTE SE6 AND GTC SPECIFICATIONS

	GTE SE6a	GTE SE6b (auto)	GTC (SE8)	Middlebridge GTE
Layout and chassis	Three-door four-seat coupé/estate. Glass-fibre body shell, steel chassis (All models)			
Engine				
Type	Ford Essex 3.0	Ford Cologne 2.8	Ford Cologne 2.8	Cologne 2.9
Block material	Cast iron	Cast iron	Cast iron	Cast iron
Head material	Cast iron	Cast iron	Cast iron	Cast iron
Cylinders	6	6	6	6
Cooling	Pressurized water and antifreeze mix	Pressurized water and antifreeze mix	Pressurized water and antifreeze mix	Pressurized water and antifreeze mix
Bore and stroke	93.67 x 72.42mm	93.02 x 68.5mm	93.02 x 68.5mm	93 x 72mm
Capacity	2994cc	2792cc	2792cc	2933cc
Valves	2 per cylinder	2 per cylinder	2 per cylinder	2 per cylinder
Compression ratio	8.9:1	9.2:1	9.2:1	9.5:1
Carburettor	Weber twin-choke downdraught	Solex-Pieberg downdraught	Solex-Pieberg downdraught	Bosch Jetronic fuel injection
Max power (claimed)	135bhp @ 5,500rpm	135bhp @ 5,200rpm	135bhp @ 5,200rpm	150bhp @ 5,700rpm
Max torque	172lb/ft @ 3,000rpm	159lb/ft @ 3,000rpm	159lb/ft @ 3,000rpm	157lb/ft @ 3,000rpm
Fuel capacity	20 gallons/91 litres	20 gallons/91 litres	20 gallons/91 litres	20 gallons/91 litres
Transmission				
Gearbox	Ford four-speed manual with optional overdrive	Ford three-speed automatic	Ford four-speed manual with optional overdrive	Ford five-speed manual/Ford four-speed auto
Clutch	Single plate, diaphragm spring	Torque converter	Single plate, diaphragm spring	Man: Single plate, diaphragm spring Auto: torque converter
Ratios				
1st	3.163:1	2.47:1	3.16:1	Man: 3.358:1 Auto: 2.474:1
2nd	1.95:1	1.47:1	1.95:1	Man: 1.809:1 Auto: 1.474:1
3rd	1.412:1 (o/d 1.098:1)	1:1	1.41:1	Man:1.258:1 Auto: 1:1
4th	1:1 (o/d 0.778:1)	n/a	1:1	Man: 1:1 Auto: 0.75:1
5th	n/a	n/a	n/a	Man: 0.825:1
Reverse	3.35:1	2.11:1	3.35:1	Man: 3.375:1 Auto: 2.111:1
Final drive	3.31:1	3.54:1	3.54:1	3.54:1

	GTE SE6a	GTE SE6b (auto)	GTC (SE8)	Middlebridge GTE
Suspension and steering				
Suspension front	Triumph-based independent double wishbone, coil springs and damper, anti-roll bar (all models)			
Suspension rear	Live rear axle, twin trailing arms and Watts linkage. Coil over dampers (all models)			
Steering	Rack and pinion. Optional power assistance (all models)			
Tyres	184HR14 radial	184HR14 radial	184HR14 radial	195VRx65x15 radials
Wheels	Steel, 5.5J (optional alloy/steel Dunlop)	Steel, 5.5J (optional Wolfrace alloy)	Steel, 5.5J (optional Wolfrace alloy)	Cast alloy 6Jx15 inch
Brakes				
Type	Disc front, drum rear	Disc front, drum rear	Disc front, drum rear	Disc front, drum rear
Size: front	10.5in diameter	10.5in diameter	10.5in diameter	10.5in diameter
Size: rear	10in diameter	10.6in diameter	10in diameter	10in diameter
Dimensions				
Track: front	58.14in/147.7cm	58.14in/147.7cm	58.14in/147.7cm	58.14in/147.7cm
Track: rear	56.13in/142.6cm	56.13in/142.6cm	56.13in/142.6cm	56.13in/142.6cm
Wheelbase	103.8in/263.6cm	103.8in/263.6cm	103.8in/263.6cm	103.8in/263.6cm
Overall length	174.5in/443.2cm	174.5in/443.2cm	174.5in/443.2cm	174.5in/443.2cm
Overall width	67.75in/172.1cm	67.75in/172.1cm	67.75in/172.1cm	67.75in/172.1cm
Overall height	52in/132cm	52in/132cm	52in/132cm	52in/132cm
Kerb weight	2,762lb/1,252.8kg	2,790lb/1,265.5kg	2,790lb/1,265.5kg	2,790lb/1,265.5kg
Performance				
Top Speed	115mph/185km/h	110mph/177km/h	116mph/187km/h	Not available
0–60mph	9.4 secs	12.3 secs	11.6 secs	Not available

BACK TO BASICS:

THE SCIMITAR SS1 (1984–1989), SST (1990) AND SS2/SCIMITAR SABRE (1992)

INTRODUCTION

Towards the end of the 1970s, Reliant's GTE and GTC were starting to look dated and proving to be less than competitive against the mainstream manufacturers' offerings. With Ford's Capri and Vauxhall's Royale Coupé (Opal Monza) providing decent four-seat coupés, and Alfa's GTV, Lancia's HPE and Datsun's 280Z representing the more overtly sporting hatchback coupés, Reliant's cars were being squeezed on both price and performance. More importantly, the

market sector that Reliant itself had created, with the original GTE, was filling up, with more and more cars competing for a limited number of buyers. Reliant may have had an impressive history as a successful niche-market player, but it was being chased out of the very niche that it had created.

The company needed to find a new gap in the sporting-car range and in the late 1970s it began to look at a successor to the big Scimitars. Market research identified a new niche: the budget small two-seat open-top sports car, epitomized by the rapidly

The SS1, or 'Small Sports 1', was Reliant's attempt to produce a replacement for the classic British sports cars from MG and Triumph, which dominated the market in the 1960s.

The complex chassis, with its fabricated central backbone, tubular outriggers and bolt-on armatures to support the body, gave the SS1 the rigidity it needed to be a car with excellent handling.

ageing MG Midget, Triumph Spitfire and MGB, and their replacement, the TR7.

Reliant had recently recruited Ed Osmond as Director of Engineering. An ex-Triumph man, Osmond had worked closely with Italian designer Giovanni Michelotti, who had been responsible for the styling of many Triumph designs from the 1960s and 1970s, including the Spitfire, Stag and Dolomite. It was natural that Osmond would go to Michelotti rather than Ogle Design for the new project. Unfortunately, while the car offered performance that was equal to the competition (although the 1.3 was a bit slow), along with a rear-wheel-drive chassis that handled well, independent suspension all round and reliable Ford engines, the looks left a lot to be desired.

THE SS1

The first iteration of the new Small Sports range was the SS1. Introduced in the spring of 1984, the front-engined, rear-wheel-drive two-seat SS1 went against the hot-hatch fashion of the 1980s, striving to give the buying public the choice of a traditional British sports car.

Chassis

The SS1's chassis was designed from the outset to take all of the car's stresses, enabling the body shell to be completely non-structural – Reliant even claimed that the car could be driven safely without any of its body panels installed. In a departure from Reliant's established practice of a relatively simple ladder-type chassis made from thick 'U' sections, the chassis had a backbone element fabricated from sheet steel. A steel 'space frame' was added to it, forming a perimeter around the sills and passenger cell and supporting the bolt-on body panels.

The central backbone of the chassis was fabricated from sheet steel, with the central element forming a rigid box and both ends of the structure splaying out in front to accommodate the engine, gearbox and suspension, and, at the rear, the differential and rear suspension mounts. Attached to each side of the central backbone there was a steel space frame, which was connected to the central backbone by four transverse chassis members.

The space frame was designed to form a perimeter around the driver and passenger, and provide secure fitting points for the door hinges, latches and the outer and top seat-belt mounts. On each side of the chassis the space frame comprised a fabricated horizontal sill with two vertical fabricated uprights, the forward one providing a secure mount for the door hinges, and the rear providing mounts for the door latches and seat-belt upper and outer mounts. The top of the rear upright was also connected to the main chassis by a complex shaped fabricated steel section, which gave rigidity to the upright and also provided the top mounting point for the rear coil over shock absorbers.

On top of the front and rear of the space frame there was an additional superstructure, described by Reliant as front and rear 'armatures', which were designed to support the front and rear of the bolt-

together body shell. The armatures were bolted on to the main four space-frame uprights and comprised a braced steel tubing superstructure with mounting points for all the main body panels. The armatures provided rigid mounting points for the exterior body panel and were sacrificial in the event of an accident – if they were damaged in an impact, they could be unbolted and either straightened or replaced without having to replace the chassis.

In view of Reliant's experience in producing chassis structures, and the slowdown in the production of the GTE, it is surprising that the company contracted the production of the chassis to a German company. From 1986, Reliant galvanized the chassis to protect it against corrosion.

Body and Interior

The SS1's body shell was designed to be resistant to minor damage, while being easy to repair in the event of a significant accident. To this end, the shell was made from fourteen main elements – the central body tub, doors, front and rear wings, bonnet and front panel, front bumper, rear deck, boot liner, boot lid and rear bumper. All these elements were bolted to the chassis or each other, and individual elements could be replaced. The boot inner panel, rear deck, body tub, headlamp panel and the doors were made from hand-laid glass-fibre-reinforced polyester resin – Reliant's traditional body material. The front and rear wings and the bumper panels were made from polyurethane plastic using a technique called 'reinforced reaction injection moulding', or RRIM, which resulted in flexible panels that could absorb minor impacts by deforming and then springing back into

their original shape. The boot lid was made from reinforced polyester to give a very rigid structure.

The bonnet was designed so that its underside would act as a fire barrier. It was made from glass-fibre-reinforced polyester resin, the same material as the body tub and other parts, but was produced using the Lotus-patented 'vacuum-assisted resin injection', or 'VARI', system. The VARI process did not require any expensive presses or metal tooling and resulted in a clean panel, with consistent resin fill and gel coat on all sides, which needed minimal work to be ready for painting and fitting.

While in theory the multi-composite construction of the SS1 made a lot of sense, in practice there was one major disadvantage: panel gaps. By their very nature, the bolted-on composite panels could not be made as precisely as pressed-steel panels and hence, to make everything fit together without rubbing, the gaps between the panels were inevitably rather wide. This did not give a good impression. In addition, the multitude of panel gaps resulted in additional styling 'lines', which detracted from the purity of the original appearance, which was already somewhat fussy.

A pair of pop-up headlights sat in the front panel, with the glass exposed, making them easy to wash. At the rear, a neatly integrated pair of light clusters were recessed in the bumper.

The interior of the SSI was a neatly integrated and modern offering. The plastic facia was a full-width design, with a rectangular black plastic fresh-air vent at each end. A neat rectangular instrument binnacle faced the driver, housing a fully up-to-date set of integrated instruments, which moved the dashboard decisively away from the 1960s and 1970s idiom of

One distinguishing feature of the SS1 was its pop-up headlights, which retracted backwards into the body. This meant that they were easy to clean, with the glass exposed, but it did not necessarily contribute much to the car's looks.

separate instruments scattered on a panel, as seen in the GTE. The instrument cluster, sourced from the Austin Metro, consisted of a speedometer and rev counter, between which nestled a fuel gauge and temperature gauge under a selection of square warning lights. In the 1300, these monitored ignition, direction indicators, main beam, hazards on, seat belts and oil pressure. A final light indicated brake fluid level low, handbrake on or pads worn. On the 1600 version there were also low oil, fuel and coolant warnings.

On each end of the dash was a rectangular fresh-air vent, and in the centre of the facia another pair flanked a digital clock. Below this was a centre console housing the minor switches and the heater controls. Below this was a DIN E slot for an optional radio or radio-cassette player. The main light switch was positioned on the left-hand side of the steering column shroud, and the two stalks controlled the lights, indicators and wipers.

The cabin was fully trimmed and carpeted and the chassis design allowed for a floor with virtually no sill below the door apertures. The seats were cloth-covered, with light grey velour centres, sporting red horizontal stripes, and darker grey outer bolsters, with thick red piping between the two. Leather facings, again with dark grey bolsters and light grey plain centres, were an option. Matching cloth inserts were placed on the sculptured plastic door trims, and dark grey carpets completed a nicely trimmed and contemporary cockpit.

The Small Sports interior was modern, neat and nicely styled, if a little too 1980s bland. This is an SST.

The hood was made from vinyl. It had a rear window that could be unzipped and a vinyl hood cover was also supplied, which covered the hood when it was down. The hood frame was bolted to the car, and two over-centre clips clamped the hood's front rail to the top of the windscreen. Opening and closing the hood was easy – although care was needed to avoid creasing the plastic rear windows – and when furled, the hood was located in a well behind the seats, giving an almost flat rear deck. Tinted glass, head restraints and electric mirrors were standard on the 1600 and options on the 1300. Electric windows, a hard top and a radio or cassette player were options on both models.

Engine, Gearbox and Final Drive

As was typical on a Reliant sports car, the company went to an outside supplier for the engine and transmission of the SS1. Initially, the car was offered with a choice of two engines, both from Ford. The Ford 'compound valve angle hemispherical combustion chamber' (shortened to 'CVH') engine was an up-to-date unit, first introduced in 1980 in Ford's Escort Mark III range, and the SS1 used it in two different capacities, 1296cc (1300) and 1596cc (1600). The engine was a 4-cylinder in-line unit, with five main bearings, a single belt-driven overhead camshaft and hydraulic tappets. The cylinder block was cast iron, the head light alloy and the unit was fitted with electronic ignition as standard. The 1300 version's bore and stroke was 79.96 x 64.52mm. It was fitted with a Ford variable venturi carburettor with manual choke and produced 69bhp. The 1600's bore and stroke

was 79.96 x 79.52mm; it had a Ford twin-venturi carburettor with automatic choke and produced 96bhp. Both engines had a compression ratio of 9.5:1. The 1600 engine was the same as those that powered the original non-fuel-injected Ford Escort XR3, and was fitted to the Ford Fiesta XR2 that was current at the time. The engine of the 1600 was pretty good, with Reliant claiming a top speed of 110mph (169km/h) and a claimed 0–60mph of around 9.6 seconds, but the 1300 was significantly slower, with a claimed top speed of around 95mph (153km/h) and 12.7 seconds for the 0–60mph. On their introduction by Ford, the engines had received a lot of bad publicity, due to excessive levels of noise vibration and harshness,

RIGHT: **Guy Betts had a lot of fun with his SS1; note the wrap-over design of the boot lid and the large rear light clusters.**
GUY BETTS

BELOW: **A boot rack gave a boost to the carrying capacity of this attractive SS1 1600.**

and most of the road tests of the SS1 also mentioned those issues.

The gearbox for the SS1 came from the Ford Sierra, with a four-speed version fitted to the 1300 while the 1600 had the five-speed version. The rear differential was also a Sierra unit.

Suspension

Delving into the modern parts bin and making use of developments in suspension technology, the SS1 had independent systems front and rear. It was developed to provide a combination of soft springs, long travel and controlled damping, very much in the Lotus idiom of suspension design.

At the front, the double-wishbone system used a pair of fabricated Vauxhall Chevette wishbones, both mounted on the chassis on bushes. The road spring sat in its usual position between the two wishbones, mounted on a rubber insulating pad top and bottom, and located by round pressings on the wishbone. The top wishbone was modified with the fitting of additional bracketry, which acted as a bell crank, enabling the front dampers to be mounted almost horizontally. This reduced the body height at the front of the car, while also allowing the use of decent-quality long travel dampers. An anti-roll bar was fitted as standard.

Relinquishing the live rear axle seen on the traditional British sports car since its inception, and carried through the Reliant sports car line to the SE6b, the SS1 adopted a thoroughly modern independent rear suspension set-up using an angled trailing arm on each side. The arms were a skewed 'A' shape, with each base of the arm pivoting on the chassis on bushes, and with the hub mounted on the apex of the 'A'. The bottom of the coil over shock was mounted close to the hub on the top of the trailing arm, and its top mount was fitted to the chassis. The drive shaft had a CV joint at each end, and was splined into a hub carrier, which bolted to the end of the arm and carried a bearing and the hub itself. An anti-roll bar was fitted, which connected both arms together, with its centre mounted on the chassis. Contemporary road tests all praised the SS1's handling and roadholding. The suspension made the car very neutral and stable, with only a slight amount of understeer when it was being pushed.

Brakes and Wheels

At the front, the SS1 had 8.9-inch (22.6cm) diameter discs with four-piston calipers from the Austin Metro, while at the rear there were 8-inch (20.3cm) diameter by 1.5-inch (3.81cm) width drums. A single rear brake cylinder operated both shoes, giving a single leading shoe effect, while the handbrake was cable operated and also acted on the brakes. The main

RELIANT SS1 SPECIFICATIONS

	SS1 1.3	SS1 1600	SS1 1800Ti
Layout and chassis	Open-topped two-door roadster with optional hard top. Fabricated steel chassis	Open-topped two-door roadster with optional hard top. Fabricated steel chassis	Open-topped two-door roadster with optional hard top. Fabricated steel chassis
Engine	Ford 1.3 CVH	Ford 1.6 CVH	Nissan 1800 Turbo CA18ET
Type	4-cylinder in line, single overhead cam	4-cylinder in line, single overhead cam	4-cylinder in line, single overhead cam, Garret T2 turbocharger
Block material	Cast iron	Cast iron	Cast iron
Head material	Light alloy	Light alloy	Light alloy
Cylinders	4	4	4
Cooling	Pressurized water and antifreeze mix	Pressurized water and antifreeze mix	Pressurized water and antifreeze mix
Bore and stroke	79.96 x 64.52mm	79.96 x 79.52mm	83 x 83.6mm
Capacity	1296cc	1596cc	1809cc
Valves	Two valves per cylinder	Two valves per cylinder	Two valves per cylinder
Compression ratio	9.5:1	9.5:1	8.0:1
Carburettor	Ford single venturi, manual choke	Ford twin venturi, automatic choke	Multiport fuel injection
Max power (claimed)	69bhp @ 6,000rpm	96bhp @ 6,000rpm	135bhp @ 6,000rpm
Max torque	74lb/ft @ 4,000rpm	98lb/ft @ 4,000rpm	143lb/ft @ 4,000rpm
Fuel capacity	10 gallons/46 litres	10 gallons/46 litres	10 gallons/46 litres
Transmission			
Gearbox	Four-speed manual	Five-speed manual	Five-speed manual
Clutch	Single plate, diaphragm spring	Single plate, diaphragm spring	Single plate, diaphragm spring
Ratios			
1st	3.58:1	3.65:1	3.59:1
2nd	2.01:1	1.97:1	2.06:1
3rd	1.40:1	1.37:1	1.36:1
4th	1:1	1:1	1:1
5th	n/a	0.82:1	0.81:1
Reverse	3.32:1	3.66:1	3.66:1
Final drive	3.92:1	3.92:1	3.92:1

hydraulics system was dual circuit and there was a vacuum operated servo fitted as standard. The 1300 was fitted as standard with 5.00x13-inch steel wheels shod with 175/70R13 radials and decorative plastic wheel trims, while the 1600 came with 5.50x14-inch alloy wheels shod with 185/60R14 radials. The larger alloy wheels were offered as an option on the 1300.

	SSI 1.3	SSI 1600	SSI 1800Ti
Suspension and steering			
Suspension front	Independent double wishbone with horizontal gas/air dampers	Independent double wishbone with horizontal gas/air dampers	Independent double wishbone with horizontal gas/air dampers
Suspension rear	Independent with trailing arm	Independent with trailing arm	Independent with trailing arm
Steering	Rack and pinion	Rack and pinion	Rack and pinion
Tyres	175/70R13 radials	185/60R14 radials	185/60R14 radials
Wheels	5.00x13in steel	5.50x14in alloy	5.50x14in alloy
Brakes			
Type	Disc front, drum rear	Disc front, drum rear	Disc front, drum rear
Size: front	8.9in (22.6cm) diameter discs	8.9in (22.6cm) diameter discs	8.9in (22.6cm) diameter discs
Size: rear	8in (20.3cm) diameter by 1.5in (3.81cm) width drums	8in (20.3cm) diameter by 1.5in (3.81cm) width drums	8in (20.3cm) diameter by 1.5in (3.81cm) width drums
Dimensions			
Track: front	51.25in/130.2cm	51.25in/130.2cm	51.25in/130.2cm
Track: rear	52in/132.2cm	52in/132.2cm	52in/132.2cm
Wheelbase	84in/213.3cm	84in/213.3cm	84in/213.3cm
Overall length	153in/388.6cm	153in/388.6cm	153in/388.6cm
Overall width	62.3in/158.2cm	62.3in/158.2cm	62.3in/158.2cm
Overall height	48.8in/124cm	48.8in/124cm	48.8in/124cm
Kerb weight	1,850lb/839kg	1,850lb/839kg	1,850lb/839kg
Performance			
Top speed	100mph/160km/h	110mph/179km/h	126mph/205km/h
0–60mph	12.7 secs	9.6 secs	7.6 secs

The Nissan Turbo engine gave a massive performance boost to the Small Sports range, and was a neat fit in the SS1's engine bay. This is Graham Fradgley's SST 1800Ti.

Guy Betts' car sitting on the historic Brooklands banking. The SS1 1800Ti was very similar in appearance to the smaller-engined cars, with little change in the specification from the 1600cc model.

GUY BETTS

SS1 DEVELOPMENTS – THE VARIANTS

Engine Changes for the SS1

The SS1 range gained a welcome performance boost in 1986 with the introduction of the Nissan 1800cc turbo engine, which powered the 1800Ti. This 4-cylinder single overhead cam unit, with two valves per cylinder, had a bore and stroke of 83 x 83.6mm, giving a total capacity of 1809cc. With a compression ratio of 8.0:1, the Nissan unit was fitted with a Garret T2 turbocharger, which boosted its power output to a mighty 135bhp at 6,000rpm and 143lb/ft of torque at 4,000rpm. This was enough to propel the SS1 into another performance class, with the top speed now a heady 126mph (205km/h) and the 0–60 a very competitive 7.6 seconds. The car was very well received by the press, and road tests indicated that the car's handling was not upset by the extra power. The general conclusion was that Reliant should have fitted the Nissan engine at the original launch of the SS1.

The final engine change for the SS1 was the replacement of the Ford 1300cc unit by the Ford 'lean burn' 1400 unit, which was new at the time. It had replaced the 1300 CVH unit in Ford UK's Fiesta, Escort and Orion in early 1986, and trickled through to the SS1 in 1987. With a bore and stroke of 77.2 x 74.3mm and a capacity of 1391cc, the engine was designed for fuel economy and fitted with an all-new cylinder head with 'lean burn' combustion chambers. The unit had a Weber carburettor and gave around 75bhp. The engine change made very little difference to the performance of the smallest SS1, and was not afforded much (if any) publicity by the company.

SS2

The SS2 was a concept car, based on the SS1 but completely restyled by William Towns. Aimed at the US market and commissioned by the US consortium Universal Motors in 1988, it featured a GM V6 engine of 3100cc and extensive reworking of the body. The lines were tidied up, and the car had much wider

The SS2 was a prototype that was aimed at the US market, and powered by a GM V6 engine. It never made it into production.

wheel arches, to cover the significantly bigger wheels that would be needed to take the proposed V8 power.

Scimitar SST (1990–1992)

In 1990, Reliant launched the SST, a new version of the SS1, with a completely reworked body shell. The SST retained the SS1's chassis and running gear but the body was a complete redesign. It reverted to a traditional tub, this time produced in two halves (front and rear) with the join in the passenger cell, which meant Reliant could bring production back in house. The restyle lost most of the fussy body lines that had been created by Michelotti and, with the front and rear wings incorporated into the overall body tub, most of the wide panel gaps caused by the separate wings of the SS1 were banished.

In the view of many observers, the SST was the car that the SS1 should have been; with much smoother lines and a single styling line running along each side of the car. With the pop-up headlamps now concealed when closed, the look was a lot less fussy and at last adhered to the three golden rules of small sports cars:

looks, performance and convenience. The car was a convincing rival to the newly introduced Mazda MX-5, then the benchmark of this type of car (and the only modern one in production).

The SST chassis was based closely on the SS1 unit, but minor modifications were made to the front and rear 'armature' superstructure, to support the new two-piece front body shell. Engine-wise, the SST continued with the SS1 range – the base model, named the Scimitar SST 1400, was powered by the Ford 1392cc CVH 'lean burn' unit, with a single overhead camshaft, which pumped out a reasonable 75bhp at 5,600rpm and 109Nm of torque at 4,000rpm. The engine breathed through a twin venturi carburettor and was fitted with electronic ignition as standard. The SST 1800Ti was fitted with the Nissan 1800cc turbo unit, pushing out a healthy 135bhp at 6,000rpm, backed up with 191Nm of torque at 4,000rpm. Fuel injection and electronic ignition provided the fuel and sparks, and both cars were fitted with 185/60 R14 tyres on alloy wheels, with the 1800Ti getting a multi-spoke design.

The SST's chassis was based on the SSI's and was galvanized as standard, to give it exceptional corrosion resistance, and comprised a fabricated steel centre tunnel with tubular steel frame to support the body shell. The body shell was produced in glass fibre and was made up of two main mouldings, split in the centre, with detachable front and rear bumper panels. The doors, bonnet and boot panels were all made from glass fibre. The all-independent front and rear suspension was carried over from the SS1.

Scimitar Sabre (1992–1995)

The final iteration of the SS1 family was the Scimitar Sabre, which was produced after Reliant was bought by Bean Industries in 1991 and first shown to the public at the 1991 Earls Court Motor Show. This was basically a re-engineered SST, with wider wheel arches and 15-inch wheels, and initially retained the Ford CVH 1.4 and Nissan 1.8 turbo engines as used on the SST.

In 1993, the Mark 2 Scimitar Sabre was announced, heralding the adoption of Rover engines in the form of the 1.4-litre K-series and the 2-litre T16 unit. Both engines were up-to-date double overhead camshaft straight-fours with four valves per cylinder, and the cars were fitted with five-speed manual gearboxes. In the event the T16 was not used in any great numbers and was quickly substituted with the well-known Nissan 1800 turbocharged unit. Production was slow and, despite a minor facelift in 1994, production finished in the following year, marking the end of sports-car production by Reliant.

The more conventional pop-up headlights of the SST cleaned up the front end and, as it tends to be dark when they are up, their appearance when in operation is not critical.

RELIANT EXPERIENCES

GRAHAM FRADGLEY – GTC AND SST

Graham Fradgley owns a 1980 GTC, a Ford Cologne V6-powered SE8, painted by a previous owner in a close approximation to Reliant's 'Buckskin Brown' with side panels in a non-standard light 'cappuccino' brown. Over the years, Graham has built up a great deal of experience of running the car, taking it to shows and RSSOC 'noggins', or meets, and using it for longer journeys, often to Shelsley Walsh Hillclimb. He finds it to be a great long-distance cruiser, with its powerful engine and good brakes, and very comfortable, particularly since he fitted a modern Ford four-speed auto box.

To complement his GTC, Graham felt the need for a smaller, high-performance Reliant. As he disliked the look of the SS1, this meant a later SST or Sabre, and he came across this one in 2008 through his membership of the Reliant Sabre and Scimitar Owners' Club. He really likes the SST, with its roller-skate ride, slightly tail-happy handling, eager performance and intimate cabin, and especially enjoys its contrast with his GTC. The car is a 1991 SST 1800Ti, powered by the Nissan 1809cc CA18ET turbocharged engine and fitted with a five-speed gearbox.

As number forty of forty-seven made, Graham's SST is a rare car. The records show that it was bought originally from a northern England Scimitar dealer via Reliant's receiver in January 1991. Since Graham has owned the car, he has treated it to various upgrades, including a new stainless fuel tank to replace the leaky original, Vauxhall Carlton ventilated front discs and Volvo brake calipers, a re-cored radiator, a rebuilt turbocharger, a new hood and replacement wheels and tyres. He has also fitted a new steering wheel, a flexible joint in the exhausts and had the web in the exhaust manifold ground out, to prevent the common problem of it breaking free and wrecking the turbo! He has also tried to make the steering lighter by fitting a replacement rack – which was partially successful – and had Gaz shocks fitted all round.

Graham finds that the SST is quick for its age, and is reasonably civilized up to about 80mph. The handling is very stable, almost go-cart like, but it can get a bit tail-happy in the wet when combined with a heavy right foot! He finds the contrast between the GTC and SST interesting; while the SST is a bit of a pocket rocket, with its Nissan turbo engine, the GTC is a great long-distance cruiser, with its four-speed auto gearbox and long-legged gait, which is comfortable but still engaging.

Graham Fradgley takes time out to admire the lines of his SST.

ABOVE: **The SS1 may have been a bit of failure when it came to sales, but in the right place it can look good.**
GUY BETTS

The front end of the SS1 1800Ti is impressive.
GUY BETTS

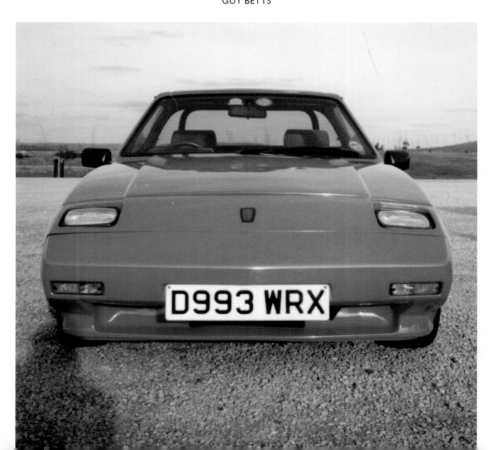

SMALL SPORTS SUMMARY

While the Small Sports project produced a neat, fine-handling traditional British sports car, which, with the Nissan turbo engine, had class-leading performance, the SS1 was never the success that Reliant had hoped for. While the company had expected to sell up to 2,000 cars a year, even with the successful restyle of the SST, poor sales sounded the death knell for Reliant's Small Sports range.

RELIANT SMALL SPORTS SPECIFICATIONS

	SST 1.4	SST 1800Ti
Layout and chassis	Open-topped two-door roadster with optional hard top. Fabricated steel chassis	Open-topped two-door roadster with optional hard top. Fabricated steel chassis
Engine	Ford 1.4 CVH	Nissan 1800 Turbo CA18ET
Type	4-cylinder, in line, single overhead cam	4-cylinder in line, single overhead cam, Garret T2 turbocharger
Block material	Cast iron	Cast iron
Head material	Light alloy	Light alloy
Cylinders	4	4
Cooling	Pressurized water and antifreeze mix	Pressurized water and antifreeze mix
Bore and stroke	77.24 x 74.30mm	83 x 83.6mm
Capacity	1392cc	1809cc
Valves	2 valves per cylinder	2 valves per cylinder
Compression ratio	9.5:1	8.0:1
Carburettor	Weber twin choke	Multiport fuel injection
Max power (claimed)	75bhp @ 6,000rpm	135bhp @ 6,000rpm
Max torque	80lb/ft @ 4,000rpm	143lb/ft @ 4,000rpm
Fuel capacity	10 gallons/46 litres	10 gallons/46 litres
Transmission		
Gearbox	Five-speed manual	Five-speed manual
Clutch	Single plate, diaphragm spring	Single plate, diaphragm spring
Ratios		
1st	3.65:1	3.59:1
2nd	1.97:1	2.06:1
3rd	1.37:1	1.36:1
4th	1:1	1:1
5th	0.82:1	0.81:1
Reverse	3.66:1	3.66:1
Final Drive	3.92:1	3.92:1

Mediocre looks and engines meant that the total number of SS1s produced over the five years (1984–1989) of production was a mere 1,507, plus fourteen prototypes. The SST family, despite its good looks, was even less successful, with only forty-four SSTs and fifty-nine Scimitar Sabres produced between 1990 and 1992. As far as can be ascertained, about 100 Mark 2 Scimitar Sabres were produced between 1993 and 1995, with about 10 per cent of the issued Mark 2 chassis numbers being incomplete.

	SST 1.4	SST 1800Ti
Suspension and steering		
Suspension front	Independent double wishbone with horizontal gas/air dampers	Independent double wishbone with horizontal gas/air dampers
Suspension rear	Independent with trailing arm	Independent with trailing arm
Steering	Rack and pinion	Rack and pinion
Tyres	185/60R14 radials	185/60R14 radials
Wheels	5.50x14in alloy	5.50x14in alloy
Brakes		
Type	Disc front, drum rear	Disc front, drum rear
Size: front	8.9in diameter discs	8.9in diameter discs
Size: rear	8in diameter by 1.5in width drums	8in diameter by 1.5in width drums
Dimensions		
Track: front	51.25in/130.2cm	51.25in/130.2cm
Track: rear	52in/132.2cm	52in/132.2cm
Wheelbase	84in/213.3cm	84in/213.3cm
Overall length	153in/388.6cm	153in/388.6cm
Overall width	62.3in/158.2cm	62.3in/158.2cm
Overall height	48.8in/124cm	48.8in/124cm
Kerb weight	1,850lb/839kg	1,850lb/839kg
Performance		
Top speed	100mph/160km/h	126mph/205km/h
0–60mph	12.7 secs	7.6 secs

CHAPTER 7

OWNING AND RUNNING A RELIANT SPORTS CAR

INTRODUCTION

Reliant sports cars offer the enthusiast a great entry into classic-car ownership, with a marque with a proud history, rugged and robust cars, and an active and supportive owners' club. With a range of pure sports cars (SE1 and SE2 Sabre and SS series), 2+2 GTs (SE4 Scimitar Coupés), the sporting estates (SE5 GTE),

the GT Estates (SE6 GTE) and a four-seat convertible (SE8 GTC), the Reliant range offers virtually all types of traditional British sporting car, giving prospective owners a wide choice.

Probably the major issue that will affect any of the Reliant sports car family, apart from the Sabre, is the relatively low value of the cars. While prices are slowly starting to rise, for decades the Scimitar, GTE and SS1

The SS1 and GTE are very different in style and function, but both can provide sports-car performance and an economical route into classic-car ownership.

The later GTE, the SE6, was an accomplished Grand Tourer. With four adult seats and good luggage capacity, it is an ideal classic car for the person who wants to travel long distances.

have been the poor relations of the second-hand classic-car market. While low prices put the cars within the reach of many enthusiasts, they also allow the cars to fall into the hands of owners who don't want to spend any money on them. The Sabres (and Sabras) are now recognized as true classics, and prices reflect this, and the Scimitar Coupés are starting to go that way. However, the bottom end of the classic-car market is littered with very cheap GTEs and SS1s, most of which may have had a couple of careful owners, but quite a few careless ones.

When buying a Reliant sports car, it is important to weigh up the condition of the car in proportion to its price. There are plenty about in various conditions, so if you are not happy with the first one you see, there will almost certainly be another one along soon!

The usual buying advice of 'bring a buddy' applies here, as always. If the friend also has some knowledge of the car, that is a definite plus; if not, there is plenty of information in the classic press on the foibles of each model, and the RSSOC website is also a useful resource.

BODY SHELL

Thanks to the glass-fibre bodywork, which was strongly made in the first place and of course rust-free, there is no need for expensive metal bodywork repairs. However, proper repairs to a glass-fibre body shell need a certain amount of skill and care. It is not just a case of digging out cracks and filling the resultant hole with some body filler. The shells do not suffer from cosmetic or body-shell rust, so restoration costs need not be excessive on a Reliant and it is perfectly possible for the amateur to achieve good-quality body repairs.

The condition of the gel coat is important, as this forms a waterproof barrier under the paint. Cracks in the coat are not uncommon, and need to be properly ground out and repaired in the correct way – simply filling a crack may work for a short time, but it will inevitably reappear. Grinding out the damaged area and applying resin and glass-fibre tissue should ensure that the problem does not re-occur. Poor repairs will always show through a new paint job after a while, usually as the repair 'sinks', so not only do any repairs need to be done properly, they also need to be allowed to cure fully before painting. Curing is a black art – it depends on the resin mix and the ambient temperature and can take days or weeks.

Structural repairs to glass fibre usually entail the grafting on of a new body section to replace a damaged section. Joining the old to the new is an exact science, and the process of attaching the new panel should be followed very carefully, to ensure the structural integrity of the overall shell and to avoid issues with the join lines appearing later. Most glass-fibre suppliers will provide instructions and books on how to do it properly. Although the glass-fibre parts will of course be rust-free, it is vital to check out where there is steel reinforcing in the body; if the glass fibre has cracked and let in water, the steel will have rusted and 'blown' the glass fibre around it. While this type of damage is not difficult to repair, it can be hard to find replacement steels to bond back into the shell.

Finally, if you are looking at a GTE, and it has a sunroof, make sure that the structural integrity of the roll-over bar in the 'B' pillar has been maintained. The original fitment fabric roof had a substantial wood and metal frame around the opening and any later replacement should have the same if it extends behind the line of the 'B' pillar.

Owners should also be aware of the cost of a proper respray, the majority of which will be spent on the preparation of the shell before any paint goes on. Preparation is much more important on a glass-fibre-bodied car, and it is vital to use a paint shop that understands this, otherwise you will be wasting your money. A good-quality respray on a Reliant will be significantly more expensive than one on a steel-bodied car, due to the extra time needed. Before agreeing to buy a car, it is well worth investigating the quality of its paint job; you want to avoid paying top price for something that has just had a quick blow-over in 'resale red'.

CHASSIS

While some of the late cars (GTE SE6, GTC SE8 and SS1/SST) had a galvanized chassis, earlier cars could now be suffering from significant rust in their chassis – hardly surprising, as some are at least thirty years old. While chassis repairs are relatively easy and straightforward, and some new chassis are available, they do tend to involve some major welding. The outriggers are the first place to go on the chassis and it is possible to carry out localized repairs on these areas with the body still attached. However, if any more extensive repairs are deemed necessary, with a significant amount of welding, the body will have to be taken off – the shells are inflammable and, once a fire gets going, it will be difficult to stop.

ENGINE, GEARBOX AND FINAL DRIVE

The Ford engines used in the cars are universally reliable, although spares for the earlier straight-four and straight-six units are becoming scarce. The Essex and Cologne V6s are strong and robust units, which will give long service, and there are many independent dealers who can supply spares and have the know-how to rebuild them.

The main problem with the early Ford engines tends to be old age. Apart from the fibre timing gears on the Essex V6s, most of which will have been replaced by now, the engines can continue to run even when virtually worn out. Old age will be betrayed by valve guide, bore and bearing wear. Worn bores will result in blue smoke in the exhaust, which indicates that the engine needs a re-bore or a top-end overhaul. If the valve guides are worn, it is pretty likely that the bores are too; apart from this, bore wear can be assessed with the heads off. Excessive oil in the breather system is a reliable indication of this type of wear. Problems with the bottom end are relatively easy to diagnose – the oil-pressure gauge will read low, oil pressure will be slow to rise on starting and quick to fall when the engine stops, and the bearings will rattle from cold starts.

The later Ford CVH units in the SS cars are also reliable, if a bit rough, and there is still good spares availability. There are a number of knowledgeable specialists who can assist with a rebuild – the need for this will be indicated if the engine is smoking or the bearings rattle on start-up.

The Nissan turbo unit in the SS1/SST 1800Ti is strong and reliable; the only weak point is in the exhaust manifold, where a divider in the end can break free. If this happens, it will wreck the turbo; the cure is to get it cut out.

Gearboxes and rear axles in the Sabres, Scimitars and GTE rarely give problems and again have reasonable spares availability. The Sierra-derived gearbox and differential in the SS models are strong and reliable. As with the engines, the main issue will be old age, so the prospective buyer should look for oil leaks and noises – all the units should be quiet – and, in the case of gearboxes, make sure that the change is not notchy or obstructive and that it does not jump out of any gear.

BRAKES

The brakes used on all the Reliant sports cars are proprietary units, which are reliable and long-lasting in service. If the car pulls to one side, it is likely that a caliper is seized and will need rebuilding. A soft pedal may indicate wear in the master cylinder but other than that there are few issues. Some owners, especially of the later GTEs, have upgraded their brakes with various aftermarket units; the internet or the RSSOC forum are probably the best arenas to see what is currently available.

SUSPENSION

The front suspension bushes on the Sabres, Scimitars and GTE/GTCs should be treated as a consumable item, as they do wear. They will cause some nasty handling traits when worn, but again are relatively cheap and easy to replace. The various bushes and swivels on the front suspension were taking increasingly heavy loads as the cars evolved from the SE4 through the SE5 and on to the SE6/8, so the later cars need more care and attention. Otherwise, the underpinnings of the cars are pretty reliable, with the only other wearing items being the shock absorbers and the various bushes used in the rear suspension links and Watts linkage. These have a reasonable long life on the cars, although the fore and aft Ballamy-Reliant links on the Sabres and early Scimitars do take a lot of strain and should be inspected and replaced more regularly. On the SS1, the suspension front and rear seems to be long-lasting and trouble-free, but obviously should be inspected for wear on a regular basis.

An SS1 at the RSSOC Sprint in 2017. The model offers a cheap way into classic motoring and many, like this one, are used as track cars.

THE FORD RS200 – BUILT BY RELIANT

Reliant did build one other sports car – the special World Rally Championship (WRC) Group B RS200 rally car, for Ford. Designed by Ford, styled by Ghia and build by Reliant, the glass-fibre-bodied RS200 had a fabricated sheet-steel chassis. It was powered by an 1803cc turbocharged 4-cylinder double overhead cam four-valves-per-cylinder Ford Cosworth BDT engine, with four-wheel-drive transmission. The engine was mid-mounted behind the driver's cockpit, and the gearbox was at the front, to give good weight distribution. All-independent suspension, with double wishbones and spring damper units on all four corners, made the car handle brilliantly, but the turbocharged engine was lag-prone; even though it produced a competitive power of between 350 and 400 horsepower, the car was difficult to drive well.

A strict two-seater, the RS200 was manufactured between 1984 and 1986, and was designed to compete against the MG Metro 6R4, Audi Quattro Coupé, Lancia Delta and Peugeot 205 T16. The car's best place in the WRC Group B class was third in the Swedish rally in 1986, but, at the end of that season, the class was abolished by the WRC governing body, the Fédération Internationale de l'Automobile (FIA). This was a result of the public outcry against the high performance of the cars competing in the class, which followed a major accident at the Rally Portugal, involving a RS200, in which three spectators were killed and many more injured. After the ban, many RS200s were used in the FIA's European Rallycross series, with the car driven by Norwegian Martin Schanche winning the 1991 title.

To meet homologation requirements, Reliant had made 200 complete cars plus spares. Reliant was responsible for building the glass-fibre body shell and assembling the car using components supplied by Ford. The FIA regulations stipulated that the cars that were built for rallying had to be road-legal – as a road car today, the RS200 provides an exciting high-performance vehicle with the added bonus of rarity.

The Ford RS200 was built by Reliant for Ford as a Group B rally car. With four-wheel drive and a Cosworth turbo engine, its performance was spectacular.

On the track, the SS1 offers pin-sharp handling and potentially a great deal of performance.

ELECTRICAL SYSTEM

Another area that will almost certainly need attention on a used Reliant is the electrics. Glass-fibre cars always suffer from poor earths, which can exhibit all sorts of strange problems, and the electrical systems of all the cars are getting old. Corroded connectors, broken switches and worn-out components can make it difficult to diagnose some of the issues. However, the inherent simplicity of the electrical system when compared to a modern car means that most (if not all) problems can be sorted out without too much expense.

All in all, the Reliant Sports car family offers a relatively low-cost entry into the classic world. The cars are perfectly capable of covering high mileages in modern conditions reliably and comfortably, as long as they are properly looked after.

THE OWNERS' CLUB FOR SPORTING RELIANTS

The foremost club for Reliant and Middlebridge sports-car owners is the Reliant Sabre and Scimitar Owners' Club, or RSSOC. Run by an enthusiastic committee, the club has a strong online presence (scimitarweb. co.uk) and also produces a bi-monthly A5 format magazine, *Slice*, which has won *Classic Cars* magazine's Best Car Club Magazine award. The technical knowledge in the club is outstanding and, with nominated model specialists for all of the Reliant and Middlebridge sports cars, owners have access to plenty of sources of information. This knowledge is backed up by the members' forums on the website and the club's collection of technical manuals and data, which includes a guide to alternative parts for the GTE family of cars.

The club is very active in the 'real' world, with local 'noggins' or meets (usually in friendly pubs) every month, as well as appearances at formal stands at shows (local and national) and national and international meets. The sporting side of the club has a very active competitors' section, which oversees the running of regular sprints and hillclimbs around the country, as well as supporting regular Autotests. With its blend of social, competition and technical aspects, the club offers something for everyone and plenty of opportunities to meet other like-minded members and see other Reliants and Middlebridges. Finally, the club also has access to some special motor insurance schemes at discounted rates.

The RSSOC is an exceptional club. The committee members are knowledgeable and only too happy to promote their cars, and their knowledge has contributed greatly to the content of this book. After meeting with many club members, at 'noggins',

The RSSOC holds many meets through the year. This lovely Scimitar Coupé was seen at the Culborough event in 2017.

individually and at club events, I came to the conclusion that it would be hard to find a more enthusiastic, friendly and welcoming group. The club also has a close and useful relationship with Graham Walker Ltd, a company based in Cheshire that keenly supports all things related to the Reliant sports car. The company bought up most of the remaining stock when Middlebridge was closed down, and carries a wide range of spares for all the sporting Reliants. They also support the owners' club, and will usually have a stand at the main RSSOC events throughout the year.

The SS1 is starting to attract serious collectors – this immaculate CVH-engined example was exhibited at the RSSOC Sprint in 2017.

RELIANT EXPERIENCES

SABRE ENTHUSIASTS – JOHN AND RICHARD VALLER

John Valler and his son Richard are custodians of an important and historically significant collection of Sabres, both 4- and 6-cylinder models, which fully illustrate the design and development of the first of the Reliant sports-car family. The collection comprises 7947 WD and 7946 WD, the first two UK-market right-hand-drive Sabres, which were shown at the 1961 London Earls Court Motor Show; 42 ENX, a much-rallied ex-works 1962 Sabre powered by the Ford 1703cc 4-cylinder engine; 419 EFH, a 1963 Sabre Six; and AKK 45B, another 1964 Sabre Six.

The Vallers were first introduced to the Sabre by John's father, Roger, sadly now deceased, who was a stalwart of the Reliant Sabre and Scimitar Owners' Club. Roger was responsible for rescuing many Sabres from barns and fields over the years and also rallied 42 ENX extensively after its restoration. John and Richard are carrying the tradition forwards, and preserving their examples of the Sabre family. Roger first became interested in the Sabre after buying an SE5 GTE and joining the RSSOC, where he found out about the Sabre. He was intrigued by the car, as the first example of a Reliant sports car and a direct ancestor of his GTE, and began looking for a restoration project. When 7947 WD came up, in 1978, he bought it. The car had no steering linkage – indeed, it needed literally everything doing to it – but, rather than putting Roger off, it piqued his interest in the early Reliants. The car gained later GTE wishbone front suspension during the 1978 restoration and had a period high-performance Raymond Mays alloy cylinder head fitted. Once restored, it was driven by Roger and his son John, who found that the Mays head gave decent power from the Ford engine, and that the later suspension gave predictable and well-mannered handling.

At the time of writing, 7947 WD is all in one piece and is currently undergoing light restoration before being exhibited at future RSSOC Sabre meetings. John and Richard have accumulated all the parts needed to return the car's suspension to its original 'flailing arm' specification and will be putting the running gear back to standard 1961 specification in the near future. However, they will be retaining the Mays head, as a nod to the heritage of the car, which was raced in the 1960s with just such a head fitted.

**Now restored and preserved by the Valler family, the Sabre Four
with the registration number 42 ENX was one of the works rally cars.**

(continued overleaf)

SABRE ENTHUSIASTS – JOHN AND RICHARD VALLER

In August 1980, Roger bought the ex-works Sabre 42 ENX, which had lain derelict in a field in Suffolk. After restoring the car, he used it to compete in events during the 1980s, starting with the 1982 RAC Lombard Golden 50 event, where, with Roger driving and Geoff Cooper navigating, it came twenty-eighth out of sixty entrants. Roger continued to compete in the car during 1983, entering various RSSOC hillclimbs and sprints, and coming ninth in class in the 1983 Coronation Rally. John took over driving duties from 1984, when the car came second in class in the 1984 Coronation Rally, but, in 1985, after competing in the Welsh Rally demonstration at Cardiff Castle, he had a major crash in the 1985 Coronation Rally. Luckily, no one was hurt, but the car needed a major rebuild, which was carried out during 2000–2001. It was competing again in the 2001 and 2002 Rally of the Tests, where, with John driving and Geoff Cooper navigating, it came in seventh in class at both events.

At the time of writing, 42 ENX is on the road and, while modified, it is still very original and is representative of the Reliant rally cars of the 1960s. John and Richard both enjoy driving the car, finding it quick and reasonably comfortable; once the idiosyncrasies of the leading-arm suspension are understood, the handling and roadholding are pretty good. John likes the car, as it is a strong and attractive-looking vehicle that can be used for both pleasure and competition use. He also likes the attention it draws from people, especially those who do not recognize the make, and the surprised reaction he gets when they find out it is a Reliant!

The second Motor Show Sabre, 7946 WD, was also bought by Roger in 1979, after being rescued from a barn in Scotland. While largely complete, it is currently stored in pieces, with a view to fully restoring in the future.

**John and Ricard Valler pose beside their Sabre Six
419 EFH. Behind is the ex-works Sabre Four, 42 ENX.**

The 1963 Sabre Six, 419 EFH, was inherited in March 2017 from Geoff Cooper, who had acted as navigator in many rallies with the Vallers, after he passed away. While the car was up and running when acquired, John and Richard have been busy getting it back in period trim, and have installed original Aero-style seats to replace the modern units that had been fitted, replaced missing interior trim and repainted some parts. They have also serviced the car, and replaced some minor worn mechanical parts and are just now getting down to fine-tuning and setting it up to be a reliable and relatively quick example.

The Sabre Six AKK 45B currently undergoing a full restoration was purchased by Roger in 1978; its restoration has included the fitting of a Mays head and triple Webers. John competed in the car in the 1980s and 1990s in various hillclimbs, sprints and rallies. With John driving and Geoff Cooper navigating, the car came first in class in the 1990 Illuminations Rally, and in the same event the following year the same pairing came fourth. In 2004, with John driving and son Richard navigating, the car ran in the Regis Rally, coming first in class. In the following year's Regis, the car unfortunately failed to finish due to a fuel-supply failure, and was taken off the road for a full restoration in 2006.

Today, Sabre Four 42 ENX and Sabre Six 419 EFH are on the road, Sabre Six AKK 45B is undergoing a soon to be complete full restoration, 7947 WD is complete and awaiting restoration work to commence, and 7946 WD is complete, but currently stored in pieces, awaiting the start of a restoration. All in all, the Vallers have plenty of work to do and plenty of very deserving projects, and it is great to see that the heritage of the early Reliant sports cars is in such capable and enthusiastic hands.

**With its striking paint job, 42 ENX still looks
the part as a competitive historic rally car.**

(continued overleaf)

ABOVE: **The Sabre Six is still a good-looking car and, with its rally specification, 419 EFH is quick and competitive.**

BELOW: **The interior of Sabre Six 419 EFH is designed for classic rallying while preserving the original instrument binnacle and dashboard.**

RESOURCES

ONLINE

There are many useful websites relating to the Reliant sports car. This is a selection of those that I have found most useful:

scimitarweb.co.uk: Reliant Sabre and Scimitar Owners' Club home page, with lots of
   useful links and information on the club, cars and events as well as an excellent forum.
sporting-reliants.com: run by Dave Poole, Sporting Reliants is a great resource for information
   on the Reliant sports cars.
grahamwalkerltd.co.uk: Graham Walker's company website, with lots of useful information
   about the sporting Reliant, as well as parts catalogues and ordering details for spare parts.

BIBLIOGRAPHY

There are a small number of books written about Reliant sports cars and a few more covering the whole gamut of Reliant production, especially the three-wheelers.

Chapman, Giles, *The Reliant Robin – Britain's most Bizarre Car*, The History Press, ISBN 978-0-7509-6759-4
   While it concentrates on the three-wheelers, this book does have some information about the sports cars
   and the company history.
Clarke, R. M., *Reliant Scimitar 1964–1982*, Brooklands Books, ISBN 0-907-073-670
   A collation of road tests from the contemporary press, which covers the Scimitar Coupé, GTE and GTC.
Payne, Elvis, *The Reliant Motor Company*, Nostalgia Road, an imprint of Crécy Publishing, ISBN 9781908 347367
   An excellent history of the Reliant company.
Pither, Don, *The Scimitar and its Forebears*, Court Publishing, ISBN 0 9530721 4 2
   Don Pither was a well-known expert on the Reliant sports cars, and this book, now out of print, is an
   excellent history of the cars.
Pither, Don, *Reliant Sports Cars*, The History Press, ISBN 978 0 75245676 8
   A well-illustrated history of the Reliant sports cars.
Practical Classics and *Car Restorer*, *Scimitar Restoration*, Kelsey Publishing, ISBN 1 873098 20 0
   A compilation of a number of articles covering various restoration activities of a GTE, as well as some on
   the Scimitar GTE.
Wilson-Hall, John, *Reliant Three-Wheelers: The Complete Story*, The Crowood Press, ISBN 978 1 84797 806 6
   A useful history of the three-wheelers.

INDEX

Ackermann 72
Alexander Engineering 26
Alfa Romeo GTV 98
Alfa Romeo Gulietta 23,32, 34
Alford and Alder 36,48, 72
Alpine Rally 9, 40
Alvis 86
Anne, Princess 13, 47
Ashley 7, 18, 20, 21, 22, 23, 26
Astle, Derrick 40
Aston, Bob 37, 40
Audi Quattro 118
Austin 11, 12, 13
Austin cars:
    A40 31, 34
    A60 30
    Metro 101, 104
    Seven 11, 12, 13
    Westminster 26
Austin Healey 30
Autocars 9, 12, 13, 19, 20, 22, 30, 31, 33, 42, 43
Autocars cars:
    Carmel 13,19, 30
    Sussita 13, 19, 30
    Sabra 6, 8, 9, 13, 14, 19–31, 33–37, 41–43
Avonex 18

Ballamy, Les 6,19, 20, 21, 22, 27, 28, 31, 52, 54
Baxter, Raymond 40
Bean Industries 18, 109
Bentley 44, 86
Bertone 16
Boam, Peter 94

Bond 15, 47
Borg Warner 72, 78, 84
BRM 54

Carlotti 25
Clark, Roger 40
Cooper, Geoff 122, 123
Cooper, Gerry 40
Coronation Rally 122
Cosworth 118
Crellin, Ron 40
Crosthwaite, John 54, 92

Dixon, Roy 40

Earls Court (London) Motor Show 6, 9, 13, 22, 32,
    33, 44, 46, 54, 62, 63, 72, 91, 109, 121
Easton, Peter 37
Edinburgh, Duke of 46, 47

FIA 118
Fiat X1/9 16
Fischer, Tony 40
Ford 13, 19, 26, 30, 33, 34, 52 54, 60, 72, 78, 94,
    99, 102
Ford vehicles:
    Capri 79, 98
    Consul 9, 22, 26, 27, 31, 33, 54
    Corsair 30
    Cortina 30
    Escort 69
    RS200 118
    Sierra 31, 103

Transit
XR2 102
XR3 7, 102
Zephyr 9, 33, 42, 52, 58, 60, 71, 86
Zodiac 9, 33, 55, 71
Ford engines:
CVH 102, 104, 107, 109, 112, 117
Four Cylinder 6, 8, 9, 26, 42
Straight Six 6, 9, 13, 33, 38, 42, 43, 49, 53, 54, 60
Essex V6 6, 10, 14, 53, 54, 58, 60, 71, 78, 84, 96, 116
Cologne V6 6, 87, 91, 94, 95, 96, 110, 116
Fortner, Boris 46, 47
Fradgley, Graham 11, 89, 106, 110

Gallacher, Chris 22, 38, 39
General Motors (GM) 107
Girling 28, 30, 53, 72, 85
Graham Walker Group 95, 120, 125
Gwent and West of England Enterprises 13

Heath, Tony and Jaki 8, 20, 31, 41
Helna Rubenstein 46, 47
Hodge, Sir Julian 13, 63

Illuminations Rally 123

JF Nash Securities 17
JAP 11
Jensen Healey 79

Karen, Tom 15, 46, 81

Lancia Beta HPE 79, 98
Lancia Delta 118
Laycock de Normanville 38, 58, 78
Le Jog 39
London–Prague 39
Lotus 100, 103
Lotus cars:
Cortina 30
Elite (Type 14) 27
Elite (Type 75) 82

Mays, Raymond 38, 121, 123
Mazda MX5 109
McCauley, John 94

McLaren, Bruce 39
McMillen, Ernest 40
Meadows Frisky 23
MG 37, 98
MG cars:
MGA 31
MGB 34, 85, 91, 99
Metro 6R4 118
Midget 99
Michelotti, Giovanni 10, 18, 47, 99, 108
Middlebridge 6, 58, 80, 94, 95, 96, 119, 120
Monte Carlo Rally 9, 40
Morris 1000 86

Nakauchi, Koji 94
NDK 19, 20
Nissan 6, 10, 104, 106, 107, 109, 110, 112, 117

Ogier, John 46
Ogle Design 6, 9, 13, 14, 15, 33, 44, 46, 48, 62, 63, 64, 81, 99
Ogle Design cars:
1.5 44, 46
Mini SX1000 44, 46
SX250 6, 13, 44, 46, 47, 48
Three Litre Scimitar By Ogle 63
Triplex GTS 46, 47
Ogle, David 13, 15, 46
Only Fools and Horses 15
Opal Monza 98
Osmond, Ed 99

Paris–Pamplona 39
Parkes, Bobby 40, 42
Pierce, Shaun 67, 76, 77
Pirelli 53, 55, 58, 72
Pither, Don 38, 76, 125

RAC Rally 9, 37, 40
Ray, Jimmy 40
Regis Rally 123
Reliant cars:
7 cwt 11
8 cwt 11
10 cwt 11
12 cwt 11
Regal 7, 12, 13, 15, 31, 87

Rebel 9, 14, 17, 44, 46, 87
Rialto 18
Robin 15, 17, 18, 47, 125
  FW7 16
  SE82 16
Reliant Sabre and Scimitar Owners Club (RSSOC)
  65, 74, 85, 88, 110, 115, 117, 119, 120, 121, 122
Riley 44, 46
Roberts, Peter 40
Rolls-Royce 86
Rover 'K' series Engine 109
Rover T16 Engine 109
Rover V8 Engine 16

San Motors 18
Schanche, Martin 118
Senior, Arthur 40
Shubinsky, Yitzhak 6, 19, 20
Six-Day War 58
Skeffingham, David 40
Sofia–Liège Marathon de la Route 40
Solex Carburettor 96
Standard Chartered Bank 17
Standard Vanguard 28
Stevens Cipher 16
SU Carburettor 27, 31, 38, 52, 60
Sunbeam 37, 86

Tamworth 11, 15, 18, 22, 30, 33
Towns, William 10, 107
Triumph 14, 36, 37, 43, 79, 83, 97, 98
Triumph cars:
  GT6 26
  Herald 26, 37
  Mayflower
  Spitfire 26, 34, 91, 99
  Stag 18, 88, 90, 91
  TR3
  TR4 36
  TR6 72, 91
  TR7 99
Tulip Rally 9, 37

Universal Motors 107
Unwin, John 17, 82, 85, 87, 88, 95

VARI 100
Valler, Roger, John and Richard 32, 33, 40
Vauxhall cars:
  Carlton 110
  Chevette 103
  Royale Coupe 98
Villiers 7
Volvo 79, 110

Warner, Graham 40
Watts Linkage 28, 38, 43, 53, 54, 61, 72, 79, 84,
  97, 117
Weber 54, 58, 60, 77, 78, 96, 107, 112, 123
Welsh Rally 40, 122
Wiggin, Ray 15, 17
Williams, Tom Lawrence 11, 15
Wilmot Breedon 23, 50
World Rally Championship (WRC) 118

Zenith Carburettor 26, 42, 58, 60
ZF Gearbox 22, 27, 33, 42, 52, 55
ZF Power Steering 84